Healing Troubled Hearts

To Jeff,
Your friendship has been a
Solid rock of encouragement
for me during these years.
I look forward to times together
in the future.
Love,
Bill

through

Exchanges with the Master

William Day, PhD, LCSW

My peace I give to you;
Not as the world gives do I give to you.

Let not your heart be troubled...

John 14:27

Healing Troubled Hearts

through

Exchanges with the Master

William Day, PhD, LCSW

Pyramid Publishers

Buffalo, Minnesota

Pyramid Publishers
1314 Grandview Circle
Buffalo, Minnesota 55313
763.486.2867
patrickday@pyramidpublishers.com

ISBN – 978-0-9851514-4-7
LCCN – 2014903285

Cover Painting by Kathy Ammon. Profile on back page
Cover Design by Stan Elder
Interior Design and Layout by
Just Ink Digital Design

Printed in the United States of America

To David McLean,
pastor, colleague, friend,
who warmly welcomed Inner Healing into our Fellowship,
who has been rugged iron sharpening mine in the heat of battle,
who has been a faithful companion through thick and thin.
David, I believe the Lord seeded this book
into our early exchanges, many years ago.
He was Present with us
as we talked on into the night.

For many years I immersed my troubled heart in humanistic psychology and New Age spirituality, desperately trying to find healing. I found one dead end after another. This book is about finding healing that finally transformed my life and the lives of others. I use the term *inner healing* to describe what happened for me, my patients, and colleagues, but I want to assure you that this healing process is neither New Age nor is it anchored in modern psychology.

If you believe in Jesus and yet have a troubled heart, I invite you to read on because this book sets forth His Gospel, His ministry, and His healing for troubled hearts—expressed in the testimonies below. I also invite all who are interested in knowing more about the true ministry of Jesus. Who He is and what He does is the heart of this book.

Bill Day

What recipients of healing are saying...

"Inner healing ministry has taken me spiritually where Bible intake and traditional counseling simply could not. As a pastor, I whole-heartedly affirm the dire need for solid Bible teaching and other conventional spiritual disciplines, but I now see inner healing as an incredibly valuable aspect of the sanctification journey. Through inner healing, I have come to truly know God as Father, to recognize the voice of my Shepherd, and to appreciate more dearly the ministry of the Holy Spirit." *GMc*

"In memory after memory, God revealed Himself and His Truth against every lie I believed in those places. Life began to flow in. Light began to glimmer. There were more and more periods of peace and buoyancy in my life. Over time the periods of peace lasted longer, as God put the pieces of my soul back together. The truths that God revealed in those sessions have not left me eight years later." *C*

"The wound for me was the absence of affirmation, and this showed up in many ways in my life. I could tell myself scripture to the contrary but the part of me that was carrying that pain felt shamed sadness and hopeless despair....I experienced the Lord actually come to that part of me in a session. He did many things: He spoke truth...He showed me

His perspective, and He let me experience His joy for me. It was very deep." *KP*

"It is likely that I would be in a mental hospital somewhere now but for the grace of Jesus and His inner healing of the lies I believed about myself and my life. He exchanged them for His truth about me, that I am his beloved and valued child and that He has a good plan for my life." *JD*

"I had experienced several traumatic events during my life. But over the years I learned to repress the painful memories. In order to survive, I built a firewall around myself....My memories will always be with me, but the way I experience them has changed. They no longer hold me hostage. My relationship with Jesus has changed completely since I have experienced inner healing. He no longer seems remote and abstract to me. He is my companion and my friend. I can feel his presence. He is the LIVING God." *AK*

"What really blew me away about inner healing was that God speaks at all. I didn't believe in that and I didn't trust most people that said they did. But I have no doubt that He spoke to me personally about me and it changed my relationship with Him and the way I practice my faith." *JC*

Preface

For a long time I have believed that there is an inner freedom-space within each of us; the power of human choice lives there. When this space is trespassed or violated in some way, bad things often happen. I am sensitive about telling people how they should think because I grew up in a religious culture in which thoughts, beliefs, and doctrines were poured into my head on a daily basis. My behavior followed duty and fear rather than convictions. At age twenty-five I walked away from that way of living, never to return.

Throughout this book I describe my beliefs and convictions, but these have been tried and tested in the forge of life-experiences. I have faith but it is not blind faith, although sometimes at first I saw only dimly. However, when I repeatedly stepped out in faith and trusted my relationship with God, it became a ground of experience. Then, when my faith proved to be true, it became a way of knowing and seeing. Now my life is based on a deepened trust that has grown out of this tested faith.

The story is my narrative and that of my patients and colleagues. I invite you to read it but leave it to you to determine whether or not the accounts and views connect at all with your life and your views. In other words, I will respect your freedom-space.

Whether or not I use the first person "I," please know that I am speaking for myself. I have refrained from making *general* statements ("as we know"), or d*eclarative* statements ("this is the way it is"), or *authoritative* statements ("you should see it this way"). Sometimes I speak passionately, out of strength of conviction. Sometimes I give interpretations and judgments of texts and events. Whatever the case, I own all statements herein as my own, except where noted otherwise.

Introduction

Healing Troubled Hearts

As you read this book you may be taken into your own story of how you dealt with troubles that came into your life. My story begins with a memory of when I was in 8th grade and had the after-school chore of cleaning the blackboard. I saw the following (which I had not noticed during class) chalked in a corner of the board: "Remember that every-one you meet in life is carrying a heavy sack of rocks."

Those words have remained etched in my mind. As my own sack of rocks filled up during the ensuing decades, and as I became aware of the sacks of others, I learned the truth of that statement. But questions emerged as my load became heavier and my heart more distressed:

- These broken dreams, emotional turmoil, frustration after frustration, the dark nights of loneliness...are they burdens that belong to the human condition, and I just have to carry them and learn how to manage them?
- Why do the same feelings keep troubling me? Inner conflict, sadness, anxiety, and guilt keep churning around in my heart no matter what I do to deal with them.
- Is it possible to attain real healing, transformation, peace?

Forty-two years ago I lived in San Diego, California and was a member of a radical underground group. We talked seriously about how to overthrow the oppression that we believed had hijacked America. I had long hair and a scraggly beard, wore a wrinkled, faded-green Army jacket, and smoked marijuana on a regular basis. I was reacting to and opposing almost everything in my first twenty-seven years of life. Our underground group thought we had solutions that would transform ourselves and the world.

Today I am sitting here writing a book about a kind of transformation that is galaxies-removed from my drug-fogged rebel days 40 years ago. It has been a wild ride and has taken a long time, but I have answered some of the questions above and want to share the results of my search with you.

Perhaps you are on a quest of your own, energized by unresolved troubles in your heart. Perhaps you are a minister or counselor...God has used you to help others but you want to keep learning how to be of service. Perhaps you are simply motivated by the hunt for that most elusive prey—truth. Whatever the case, if the questions above resonate with issues that affect you, I encourage you to walk a few steps with me to see if my discoveries interest you.

Exchanges with The Master

Exchanges. A first meaning is simply the dialogue of speaking and listening that happens in personal encounters. Important as that interaction is, the aspect of exchange that I will mostly develop is the process of releasing something and receiving something else in return. To exchange has a kind of *total* connotation, in that something is completely handed over and, as part of the same dynamic, something else comes to take its place. The stories in this book are full of changing out and replacing—similar to breathing out carbon dioxide and breathing in oxygen. The exchange-process is all around us in many forms and on many levels; the focus in this book will be on exchanges that take place within soul and spirit levels of human life.

The Master. I have had many masters, lords, and taskmasters in my life, and now I have one Master: the Lord Jesus. The understanding that frames all of my statements about Jesus is that God, the Creator of all, spoke Himself into human history in a unique way, in a unique event, in a personal Presence, in His Word made flesh, 2000 years ago.

This book is an expression of the historical reality of Jesus' resurrected Presence in human lives. I know Him as Savior and as King, yet I also know him as Brother and Friend. Alongside the stories of how I came to know Him in these ways, I present stories of patients and colleagues—taken from actual healing sessions. All of these accounts together have shaped a core of confidence prompting me to write this book. I am convinced that God passionately yearns to speak His healing truth into human hearts.

Clarifications

1. I have been given permission to disclose the contents of the therapy sessions I use, but names and some personal details of patients and colleagues have been changed.
2. Out of respect I capitalize God and pronouns referring to Him. I also sometimes capitalize His attributes, such as *Love, Presence,* and *Life* as a way of expressing my belief that He personally inhabits extensions of Himself into our lives. I don't believe He parcels out impersonal "forces" of Himself; rather, He relates person to person.
3. Although I freely quote from the Bible and reference the origin of the quotes so you can search for yourself, in the text of any given chapter I don't always reference authors from whom I have adapted ideas. I do this to keep the flow of the narrative relatively free. I acknowledge all my sources directly in the AFTERSTORY following PART III.
4. Disclosure Statement: Although I freely share interventions and strategies for dealing with emotional and spiritual issues, this book is neither a formal treatment manual nor is it a training program. Readers are cautioned about the potential risk of using limited knowledge when integrating any new method into practice.

Overview

PART I. The first three chapters are a biographical sketch of my quest for healing and freedom. The next five chapters detail how my personal transformation merged with professional training as I learned to facilitate healing for others.

PART II. Chapter Nine focuses on the necessity for healing and transformation. I draw conclusions from years of wrestling with my own issues, from interacting with hundreds of patients, from exchanges with colleagues and mentors, and from interrelating with the Word of God. Chapter Ten is the heart of the book: It underscores how the ministry of Inner Healing grows out of and is an intrinsic part of the ministry of Reconciliation.

PART III. The final twelve chapters lay out the specifics of Inner Healing ministry. I start with a list of what Inner Healing is *not* and then describe its unique features and procedures.

AFTERSTORY. This is an acknowledgment of the formative, shaping, and mentoring influences that constitute the wider context of authoring this book. I give credit where credit is due and give descriptions of and directions to significant persons, training programs, books, and other resources.

CHAPTER CONTENTS

PART I
From Lost to Found: A Story of Healing and Transformation

PART II
From Brokenness to Wholeness: Foundations of Restoration

PART III
Exchanges for a Lifetime: The Ministry of Inner Healing

   - Dealing with the Demonic
   - The Power of Addiction
   - A Malevolent Myth of Masculinity
   - Inner Healing for All Occasions

The Shaping of *Healing Troubled Hearts*

PART I
From Lost to Found: A Story of Radical Transformation

Chapter 1

Life Begins in a Bubble

My parents were devout Roman Catholics and before I came along they were practicing the rhythm method of birth control to avoid having another child. Times were tight economically and my father thought that two children were enough. At the same time my mother was secretly praying for the favor of a child. Within this ambivalence I was conceived and was born in February, 1942.

Soon after my birth, my maternal grandmother came for a visit and informed my parents that she had a dream in which it was revealed to her that I had a special destiny in life. My parents and extended family embraced her dream as pointing to what they thought of as a "special destiny" for an Irish Catholic son. When I was two weeks old my maternal uncle, a Catholic priest, laid me on the stone altar at Holy Rosary Church in Detroit Lakes, Minnesota, dedicated me to the Blessed Virgin Mary, and proclaimed that my destiny in life was to be a Catholic priest. It was a simple ritual but one that had ramifications far beyond what anyone could have anticipated at the time.

Special but Alone

Growing up I did not have a thought of becoming anything other than a priest and I accepted that this was my destiny. On one hand I had a sense of belonging to an elite group, a sense of being special, of having a destiny of significance waiting for me. On the other hand I had few experiences of just being a flesh-and-blood boy, belonging to a human family.

Kind though my parents were, there was a reserve in them towards me. I experienced them more as guardians, taking care of me until it would be time for me to leave home after eighth grade. I felt different from everyone else—even my two brothers and sister seemed at arms' length to me. Being special had definite advantages—like receiving a deluxe tricycle with a big fur seat from a family friend who was a bishop in Kentucky. But there was isolation.

I did not consciously experience the isolation, but I had recurring nightmares. I would wake up in fear, screaming. My father would come and take me out into the hall, to sit in his lap under a hanging light bulb. He held me (as parent more than guardian) until I calmed down and could return to bed. I could not really describe to my father why I was so frightened. The nightmares were different each time, just daily events in life. But the feeling I had inside was the same, awful fear.

While in therapy in my thirties, a psychotherapist guided me to walk consciously into one of those nightmares, and then I "got it." In the dreams I was in a transparent bubble. I could see people, animals, etc., through the bubble, but couldn't hear, smell, or touch anything. I was alone in the bubble, and the feeling that would wake me was fear. No connection, no attachment, no sense of belonging...alone in a bubble...and it was scary in there.

In retrospect, it seems clear that the emotion in each recurrent nightmare was separation-anxiety generated from a lack of basic human attachment. This buried anxiety would burst through the lowered veil of consciousness during sleep, manifesting in fear-laced nightmares. My father physically holding me in the hallway calmed the anxiety, momentarily resolving my sense of detachment. The anxiety would abate, like stirred-up sediment in a river settling back onto a riverbed. In the morning life would return to "normal."

The First Arrow Goes Deep

In *The Sacred Romance*, author John Eldredge describes a longing in our hearts, "...to be part of something out of the ordinary....The deepest part of our heart longs to be bound together in some heroic purpose with others of like mind and spirit" (Eldredge, 1997). Growing up I felt connected to an adventure, a heroic purpose larger than myself. There was a sense of belonging, but it was in the future and experientially remote. The nightmares were regular reminders of a dark side to the adventure: heroic though the journey might be, it would be lonely.

There is also a second story in *The Sacred Romance* that runs concurrently with the longing for adventure and romance: the story of the *arrows* that have struck us all. Along with being set on a purposeful adventure from birth, a sharp arrow was shot into my heart—an arrow of anxiety from being relationally detached. It was an arrow that separated me from natural connections with people and with all the normal events a boy might have while growing up in a small Minnesota town. I was a solo-boy, and this reality would follow me as I grew into a solo-man. In my childhood I did not think of this arrow as an enemy; it was just part of the priest-adventure, and I accepted it as such. I did not know until later that this arrow would remain painfully stuck in me for many years to come.

The Seminary: A Second Arrow Also Goes Deep

My time to leave home came after finishing Catholic elementary school in 1956. I was 14 years old. My father drove me from Detroit Lakes, Minnesota to Holy Cross Seminary in La Crosse, Wisconsin, a journey of 350 miles. I remember standing in the freshman dorm, stunned, suitcase in hand, looking out at rows of 24 single beds. On the left wall there were 12 sinks, on the right wall 24 lockers. This would be home for the next eight years.

The *romance* had begun and, after the initial shock, I felt a gradual sense of belonging and connection. This was my band of brothers with whom I could bond in the high-call adventure of becoming a priest. However, the arrow of being-alone stayed firmly in place, in that we seminarians were given strict admonition against forming "particular friendships." Scripture was used to reinforce the warning. We were told that 1 Corinthians 9:22 pertained to us: "...become all things to all men." As priests we would need to be servants to all members of the flock, and therefore not be attached to any person in particular. I followed the guidelines and developed a relationship-style of aloofness.

I fully accepted my identity as a priest-to-be. This was my life. This was me. I returned home to Minnesota for vacations; but, with each passing vacation, I looked more and more forward to the end of vacation when I could return to my "real home." However, upon returning to the seminary in the fall of my junior year in college (my seventh year in the seminary), I was shocked when uncomfortable doubts about my vocation suddenly appeared. It wasn't about missing girls, or missing anything on the outside; it was more like someone had taken away a precious, shining jewel from inside of me when I wasn't looking.

I didn't know why the vocation-jewel had been removed, but it was. I no longer felt like I was supposed to be a priest, and I couldn't figure out what had happened and why. I consulted my spiritual director and other priests, all of whom tried to dispel my doubts—to no avail. I could not get my precious gem back. I had not been taught how to talk or listen to God in an informal, non-structured way, so He seemed silent and remote to me. I finished my senior year of college at Holy Cross, but all sense of *belonging* was gone. The jewel was gone, the adventure was over, and I was no longer a member of a band of brothers.

Once again I was a stranger in a strange land, but this time there was no adventure waiting for me in the future. In my perception there was nothing waiting for me. Like Adam in the Garden, I had to leave, and I felt a sense of shame...though I didn't know why there would be shame. I had been a good seminarian, but evidently something was missing. A powerful arrow of *rejection* pierced my heart but I didn't see it or feel it. It went in quickly and silently, under the radar of consciousness...and it went deep. The year was 1964. I walked out of the seminary and into the world, free from the confines of the seminary. However, I was wounded and bound up with pain, fear, and anger, a fact I didn't realize or acknowledge for a long while.

Years later, when I was finally in a healing community and ready to receive healing, I discovered that I had interpreted the loss of my vocation as a belief that God had rejected me. I believed that I was found to be unworthy, that I wasn't qualified to advance to the major seminary (the last four years of the twelve-year training). I had been cut after my eight-year stint in the "minor leagues." Deep soul-surgery would be needed to remove this embedded belief, but for now and for many years I would carry the pain, without an awareness of my rejection interpretation.

I will describe the healing balm that was eventually poured into my soul, but first come the stories of my many attempts to self-medicate the pain and loss. The seminary had been a way of life, not just a school. Gone was a sense of purpose, of belonging, and of my whole identity. I was a young man stripped of a sense of direction, and as soon as I walked outside the walls of that seminary and into the world, a cavernous sinkhole opened up inside of me.

Chapter 2

Life on the Run

A Dull Ache

Upon leaving the seminary I entered Marquette University in Milwaukee, Wisconsin and earned a Master's degree in Theology. My intention was to become a lay theologian. I went on to theology studies at the same time my Holy Cross classmates entered major seminaries across the country to take theology courses prior to ordination. I had a keen interest in philosophy and theology so it was a natural next step for me; but I think the immediate entry into graduate studies served to deaden and defer the pain. Becoming a lay theologian was the next best thing to being a priest, or so I told myself. This positive spin on my life-change kept me from admitting that deep inside I really felt it was a *distant second*.

From an early age my mind had been programmed and shaped by legalistic, conservative Catholic doctrine. I had spent my first 21 years of life learning about sin-management and examining every piece of literature and philosophy to determine whether or not it lined up with the Catholic worldview. My head was crammed with knowledge and I had learned to control my behavior...but my heart was locked up. I was penned in by *shoulds*, *oughts*, and the fear of consequences. Relationships with girls were nonexistent, and my relationships with the seminary guys had been mostly the typical male camaraderie that can so easily stay on the surface. I was athletic and academic, and those two areas formed the basis for bonding.

Life at Marquette brought a dramatic shift. The theology courses at Marquette had a liberal lean to them. The more open and liberal atmosphere helped to loosen some of my rigid thinking. I also broke into the realm of relationships by dating young women and getting to know guys who weren't seminarians, though I mostly remained inwardly detached. To help the breaking-open process, I developed an affectionate relationship with alcohol which served as a social lubricant.

I did not have a personal relationship with God. In the seminary chapel, an always-lit candle announced Jesus' presence inside a small wafer of bread in a gold container on the altar. In devotions such as the Mass, the Stations of the Cross, and the Rosary, I felt as though I was relating to God. But He was much more *out there* than *down here* or *with me*. I said the repetitive prayers and participated in liturgical services, but absent was a sense of God's indwelling personal Presence. Nothing new happened at Marquette.

There had been endless God-talk in seminary classes, retreats, and sermons, and in all these activities there seemed to be a kind of magical thinking in play—that somehow we were making God present by talking about Him...as though He lived in doctrines, propositions, and concepts. At Marquette I gradually stopped attending Mass and other liturgies, but the God-talk was accelerated to another level because *all* the courses were about Him.

I can remember feeling holy and godly because I was spending most of my time talking about God, though I didn't lead a godly life. I didn't have a clue that this was exactly why Jesus rebuked the Pharisees: they were involved not with the *living God* but with concepts, laws, and doctrines *about* God.

I was locked up by myself in my head and barely realized the state I was in, though I certainly did not feel at peace or free. My heart was so uninvolved in my life that I could not feel the hunger and thirst for real life that would later emerge. I just felt a dull ache.

The Death of God

After receiving my Master's degree I taught theology for two years—first at Portland University in Oregon, and then at Santa Clara University in California. In between those two years I married a woman who had also gone through Marquette's degree program in theology. I hadn't dated much, certainly not enough to open my locked-up heart, but at age twenty-five I thought it was time to marry. And so I married someone with whom I thought I was compatible enough to make a go of it.

My world rapidly began to unravel. Taking leading thoughts from my liberal theology at Marquette, I began to explore the many challenges to Catholic orthodoxy that were developing in the years after the Second Vatican Council ended in 1964. I wedged my mind into the cracks that began to appear in the absolute nature of orthodox doctrines, moral codes, and understandings of God.

I remember reading Bishop John Robinson's ground-breaking book, *Honest to God.* He cracked open the transcendent image of God as up-there and out-there, stating that this image was antiquated, irrelevant, and needed to "die." He referenced theologians who spoke of God as living in the here-and-now. Bishop Robinson also attacked absolute moral codes, introducing thoughts about *situation ethics* which strongly suggested that moral codes were not set in stone. Here was a respected Anglican theologian questioning orthodox Christian doctrines about God and moving toward moral relativism. My soul resonated with these stone-breaking thoughts and I eagerly adopted them as my own.

I was also drawn to the death-of-God theologians who believed that, in Jesus, God historically and forever gave up His transcendent separateness as He became totally unified with His whole creation. By the end of my second year of teaching I was well on my way to being a death-of-God theologian. I began teaching that being Christian meant being *fully human*, not realizing that I had turned the Gospel on its head. I did not even notice that "being fully human" included the human depravity so evident in the world and within me. I had tuned out this negative side of being human, no doubt driven by my growing urgency to discover what life was all about. Thinking or talking about sin seemed to be a discordant note in my current quest; the word *sin* gradually disappeared from my everyday vocabulary and from my teaching.

My status in 1968 consisted of the following:

- The rock-hard, lifeless structures of dogmas, rituals, and laws were crumbling away inside of me. More and more the Catholic Church felt like a prison, and I wanted out.

- I was moving in the direction of Friedrich Nietzsche, the German philosopher who declared the "actual" death (total irrelevance) of God.
- My rejection-wound was still below the surface, and I was not consciously trying to get away from or get even with God. I just felt an awful *deadness* inside, and I wanted *to live*. I didn't even know what being fully human meant but I wanted to find out.
- Without much calculation, and more out of urgency than anything else, I resigned my position at Santa Clara University and abandoned a career as a lay theologian. I enrolled in a Master's degree program in Social Work at San Diego State University. I didn't know what I wanted to do or become, but it looked like there were many possibilities in the field of social work. My wife had also become disenchanted with Catholicism and was willing to leave her teaching position in theology.
- I felt a huge void inside. Who was I? Where was I going? What was life all about? Where was my place in it all? I had no answers for any of those questions. However, nature does indeed abhor a vacuum and some powerful replacements would soon arrive as answers, filling the void; and I was a sponge ready to absorb.

Dropping Out

By the end of my first year at San Diego State Graduate School of Social Work, I was immersed in a new inner world in which several exchanges and replacements had filled the void. I dove into the writings of Carl Rogers, Abraham Maslow, Albert Ellis, and many others who had developed the theme of *self-actualization*. For someone who inwardly felt that his *self* had been hijacked since birth, these were initially very refreshing waters to swim in.

A basic tenet in the writings was that humans have an *inborn* nature which is essentially *good*. Evil was anything that frustrated or denied our essential self-actualizing nature—such as antiquated traditions, controlling authority, and absolute moral norms. Doing what "felt right" was deemed a higher standard of morality than external laws.

The vacuum in my emptied mind rapidly filled with these "liberating" ideas. Self-realization and self-actualization replaced the need for salvation in a flash. Catholicism had been poured into me; I had taken it on but I never really wrestled with it or willingly chose it. It was not difficult, at least consciously, to just let all the doctrines drain out and be replaced with a psychology that seemed to be healing and life-giving.

However, vague feelings of anxiety, anger, and pain were rising to the surface; I began to feel more and more uncomfortable. Before leaving Santa Clara I had been invited by friends to smoke marijuana while listening to The Doors, a musical group named after the book, *The Doors of Perception*, written by Aldous Huxley while under the influence of mescaline. I had a mind-altering experience in which my inner conditioning and programming felt temporarily suspended. I smoked marijuana a couple of times more before leaving Santa Clara. When stoned I did not feel anxiety, anger, or pain. The feeling of freedom was exhilarating and I wanted more.

More came in San Diego. Some of my new classmates did drugs and I indulged in the pursuit of freedom through chemicals. I took mescaline on several occasions and smoked marijuana on a regular basis. Expanding my consciousness through drugs seemed compatible with the new doctrine of self-actualization. At age twenty-six I had become a late-blooming hippie. I let my hair and beard grow long, wore a wrinkled Army-surplus jacket, and was stoned much of the time—or speeding high on amphetamines so I could stay up all night to finish term papers at the University.

To further fill the vacuum, I joined a radical underground group called E.R.O.S., which stood for Exposure to Repression, Oppression, and Suppression. We would stage sit-ins and create other oppositional actions to challenge what we thought was a conspiratorial plot by the military-industrial complex of America to restrict human self-actualization. To dismantle the "inner constrictions" that had already been planted in us, we developed *exposure-education* weekend workshops. On these weekends 50 to 100 adults would systematically expose themselves to situations that would bring out ingrained prejudices. Then, in small-group settings we would help one another renounce and revoke these "evils."

Two examples of exposure-education come to mind: spending an evening in a gay bar and then returning to our meeting place to discuss what we thought and felt while we were in the bar; and men and women together watching a pornographic film and then breaking into small encounter groups, to confront one another with any "false" shame or embarrassment that might have arisen while watching the film.

By the end of my two years in San Diego I had substantially dropped out, heeding drug-guru Timothy Leary's advice to "turn on, tune in, and drop out." I was still a part of "the system" in that I had a Master's degree in Social Work and had taken a job in the Napa County Department of Social Services in northern California. But the change-out was substantial: I had replaced the religion of Christianity with the religion of psychology (though at the time I did not think of it as a religion); through drugs my mind had been altered and my perceptions were being "cleansed"; and my racist and sexist prejudices had been exposed and deleted, or so I thought. To complete this version of out-with-the-old-and-in-with-the-new, my marriage ended after less than two years and no children. Promiscuity filled that empty space, and I thought of the new relationships as just more positive steps toward self-realization.

There were some unpleasant changes. When relationships would end (and especially if rejection or failure were involved) it would tap into the reservoir of pain hidden in my heart, and powerful emotions of anger, sadness, and fear would well up. In the safety of a humanistic psychologist's office I began to uncover the seething turmoil underneath the surface. But the therapists I saw only dealt with the immediate pain and not the deeper issues, or they provided *insight* into the issues but not *healing*. So I would get patched up and then move along to the next adventure. In 1970 the next adventure was Napa, California.

Getting Lost

Napa hit me smack in the face with a part of life I had not seen. Along with a classmate from San Diego, I was hired by Napa County to open a Child Protection Services unit. My tidy world of self-realization, expanding consciousness, and opening my "doors of perception" was soberly shaken by the reality of an alcoholic father putting out lit cigarettes on his three-year-old son's back, by parents punching and kicking their children into submission, and by the horrors of child sexual abuse. Day after day I witnessed this dark side of life, and the tools in my toolbox were inadequate to deal with any of it. I used what I had learned, applying soul-bandages here and there, and managing situations to prevent further damage from occurring. But after a year I was totally frustrated. I knew that this was not my calling in life.

There was tremendous conflict and confusion inside of me. In San Diego I had learned that self-actualization could be achieved without much conflict, that the intrinsic goodness of the human self would come through once people saw the truth and light of innate human goodness. However, in Napa, the degree and depth of dysfunction that I experienced in the abuse, the rancor, and the violence were way beyond the parameters of my academic training, my experiences, and the understanding I had developed in E.R.O.S. In my clients in Napa I witnessed extensive self-hatred, low self-esteem, despair, hopeless-ness, and other maladies of the soul. I knew that the evil I encountered there was not coming solely from external forces such as authoritarian government, the military-industrial complex, a restrictive moral code, or bad parenting. The negativity seemed to rise from within the persons themselves.

There was another complicating reality that caught me by surprise. My own unresolved pain, anger, and anxiety were triggered by exposure to daily doses of severe human dysfunction and turmoil in the lives of my clients. The net effect of this triggering was a gradual amplification of *my* inner turmoil, heading towards a breaking point. During my year in Napa I increasingly felt as though I was inside a room in which all four walls were slowly but inexorably closing in on me, and I was slowly being smothered and crushed.

The force crushing me was not just what was happening in Napa. The situation there somehow touched into the whole edifice of my biography. I had replaced and exchanged many things during my years in Santa Clara and San Diego, but the foundational structures upon which my early life had been built were not so easily dislodged.

It felt as though the enclosing walls were composed of my whole life, from birth on. All the formative forces seemed to be there as bricks in the walls: my parents; Father Tom (my priest-uncle) who dedicated me as a baby; the nuns at Holy Rosary parochial school; the priests in the parish and in the seminary; the years growing up in a small Minnesota town; the walls and halls of the seminary in Wisconsin; my training and brain formation during my first 21 years; the hundreds of Masses and liturgies I had attended—I had dealt with none of it by the changes I had made in my life. It seemed as though it was all still there on the inside, closing in on me.

A plan came together in my mind: Leave...get outside of everything I had ever been part of since birth. This took the form of selling my 1967 Ford Mustang and purchasing a one-way ticket on Icelandic Airlines from New York to Luxembourg. I had no idea how long I would be gone or if I would return. It was the strongest urgency I had felt in my short life and I moved with it. It was a simple urge: *Go...leave...now.* Given my disillusion with humanistic psychology and the inner walls closing in on me, exiting seemed my only choice. I put the plan into action and flew to Europe in 1971.

Dozing Divinity

I drifted from city to city, country to country, month after month. However, when I returned to the United States after three years, I had not found myself nor had I found peace. However, while traveling abroad, I experienced a shaft of new spiritual light coming from the New Age people I met and in the New Age gurus I listened to and read. The "light" was a broader concept of self, a *Higher Self.*

The humanistic secular *self* had turned out to be narrow and lacked the power to overcome suffering and psychological problems. I had discovered that lack of power in Napa. While overseas I cycled back to an interest in spirituality by encountering and accepting the core New Age concept: What we call *God* is everywhere, and in everyone and everything. We search all over the world (as I was doing) and right there, already inside us is this *dozing Divinity*, waiting to be discovered and awakened. In this New Spirituality view, the divine part of us is our True Self, our Higher Self. I learned that the search leading to discovery of truth was an inward journey into the vast realms of this hidden, divine, Universal Consciousness.

An image used by many New Age teachers captured the essence of this thinking: the image of a deep underground well that supposedly exists in every human soul. The bottom of each well flows into the ocean of Divinity, our true identity. It is an ocean of Universal Consciousness and we are all drops in the oneness of this ocean. As we shed false beliefs about sin, devils, and death, we can gradually find our way into this Universal Oneness. In this system of thought (and I ran across many expressions and varieties) there was no need for a Savior. Suffering and evil were seen as resulting from *ignorance*, avoidable by learning and applying *true knowledge*.

For a while I was hopeful and felt I was on track to truth and freedom. I stopped doing drugs and strove to overcome my ego and ascend into my Higher Self. Part of the appeal of this vision was that it was expressed as a solution for each individual *and* for the world at large. The New Age vision was that, if everyone made this inward journey to their True Selves, we would be able to come together in unity and solve our planetary conflicts and problems at every level.

While in India I spent time in the ashram of an Indian guru. I learned and practiced several meditation techniques, trying to see down into my inner underground well with my inner "third eye." Also, back in Europe I studied and practiced other forms of spirituality.

After three years abroad I returned to California. It was 1974. Before long I joined an esoteric community in Sacramento, whose members practiced what was called Spiritual Science. The study and spiritual exercises in this community were based on the writings of Rudolf Steiner, an Austrian clairvoyant who had written and delivered 30 books and 3000 lectures in the 1920s. Steiner adherents were called students of Anthroposophy, a word Steiner had given to his method of achieving and applying what he called *Knowledge of Higher Worlds*. Instead of claiming to be New Age, members spoke of pursuing an esoteric form of Christianity.

In 1977 I traveled again, this time to England, to study principles of Steiner's three-fold social order, planning to apply what I learned to working in the fields of organization development and counseling. I met and married a woman while studying in the Steiner community there. We had a son and named him Adam.

While in England (1977-1980) I also took classes and received therapy from the Centre for Transpersonal Psychology. Therapists at the Centre had trained in the transpersonal (higher centers of consciousness) practices of European psychiatrists Carl Jung and Roberto Assagioli. Searching for real healing was still a significant part of my search for truth because unresolved emotional upheaval in my life continued to plague me.

In 1980 my wife, son, and I returned to the United States. We started off in a Steiner community in New Hampshire. Our marriage unraveled and we divorced shortly after moving to a Spiritual Science community in Detroit, Michigan, in 1982.

More Lost than I had Planned

By 1984, my status consisted of the following:

- I was living in the Detroit area and had moved in with a woman and her three children. She too was learning the teachings of Rudolf Steiner. We were planning to marry when her divorce became final. She became pregnant and I was the father.
- I had enrolled as a student in a doctoral program for existential and transpersonal psychology. Many of my former mentors in humanistic psychology (such as Abraham Maslow) had moved beyond what they now described as a restrictive view of humanistic self-actualization. They declared that *real* self-actualization involved the small self-merging into a Higher Self; they had shed their humanistic views and were now New Age transpersonal psychologists. I decided that this was my calling in life—to become Dr. Day, a transpersonal clinical psychologist.

- I had resumed smoking marijuana on an occasional basis, trying to tranquilize the always-present anxiety that accompanied my solo-state. Meditation and Spiritual Science had not calmed the inner turmoil.

Reflecting on this time in my life, I think it was a robust round of whistling in the dark. After all my study, striving, practicing meditation, and other spiritual exercises that promised enlightenment, no significant transformation had taken place. For example, at the Centre for Transpersonal Psychology in London, a therapist had guided me into bringing my childhood nightmares into conscious awareness. But *understanding* what was going on in the nightmares neither removed the fear nor did it remove me from the bubble; part of me was still there, and I could not will myself out. I was still locked up inside myself, in a bubble of isolation.

Relationship-wise my life was a disaster. I had gone from one relationship to another, trying to remove the deep detachment-arrow that I spoke of in Chapter One. I kept trying to attach, to belong, to be close to someone. Having a situation ethics (everything is relative...no absolutes) code of morality allowed me to begin and end sexually intimate relationships at will, but such license had led neither to freedom nor to peace. Bumbling in and out of relationships, I was now headed towards my third marriage, hoping this would be the one that would close and heal the attachment wound.

In short, my life was a mess. I did not acknowledge it as such but I was treading water, hanging on, hoping that my involvements in a new relationship and a new career would get me up and swimming. Life had become more complicated and intense than ever before, with new and growing family responsibilities added to the mix. I felt weariness as well as increased anxiety creeping in as I continued treading water.

Chapter 3

Real Life Begins

First Encounter

It was late autumn, 1984, in a suburb of Detroit, Michigan. More out of curiosity than anything else, my fiancée and I had accepted our babysitter's invitation to visit a service in her church. After seven years' involvement in Spiritual Science communities in Sacramento, England, New Hampshire, and now Detroit, my interest in Rudolf Steiner's clairvoyant knowledge had waned—another light that had begun bright and dimmed with time. A new light had recently appeared in a doctoral program in existential and transpersonal psychology, and I had begun to follow that light.

I remember well that Wednesday evening service in Brightmoor Tabernacle, an Assemblies of God church. I had never been in a Protestant church before. In Minnesota we had Lutheran, Methodist, and other Protestant churches, but as a child I was taught to stay away from those "havens of Satan." So at first I felt strange sitting there, vaguely feeling the reprimand my parents would have delivered. However, those feelings were quickly dispelled as the pastor launched into the scripture of the Last Supper from the Gospel of John.

I had heard many sermons in my life but nothing like this one. The pastor skillfully opened up passage after passage, letting the theme of God's love for us exude from the words like a delicate fragrance. In those moments I was touched on the inside by something that imperceptibly made its way past my protective walls and defenses. The sermon was not a transmission of knowledge from the pastor's head to my head. His words were coming from his *heart*. I felt energized and enlivened in my heart, as did my fiancée. Driving home that evening, I realized that I had just heard the best sermon of my life.

We returned on Sunday for the full service. Although my curiosity was piqued by Wednesday's sermon, I was still wary of being in a

Protestant church. My usual mindset had settled back into defensive, critical mode, and skeptically I watched about 500 people talking in the aisles and beginning to fill the pews. I felt as though I was on the *inside* of reality, and these church folks were on the *outside*, in some weird, unreal, religious world. The service began. Within ten minutes, in an utterly surprising shift, my perception completely flipped: *They* were on the inside of something I intuitively knew was real and alive, and *I* was on the outside. In that moment, at age 42, I had my first encounter with God.

I heard a clear, authoritative, yet gentle voice. I did not hear the voice audibly with my ears, yet I somehow perceived the words within me, and they were being spoken by a person. I had a sense of a *personal presence* other than myself. It was not the voice of my self-talk chattering away as it did throughout the day. This presence was clearly *other* and *outside* of myself, yet communicating with me.

The words spoken were: "I am Life." As those words were spoken, a remarkable thing happened within me...like a fog lifting. I saw that everything I was attached to: the drugs, the hippie lifestyle, my New Age dozing divinity beliefs, my frantic search for knowledge—all of that comprised an extensive life-support "machine" into which I was plugged. I could see and feel the tangled tubes attaching me to those things, and I saw that this whole life-support system was *pseudo-life*.

Then a gentle but firm understanding came into my mind: "You must choose what to have as life—Me or the life-supports to which you are attached." The tone and meaning of the proposal were crystal clear: It was an invitation, but it was a one-or-the-other proposition. I could not have it both ways. I had to choose what would be *life* for me. There was a startled pause as I absorbed this realization. Then, inwardly, yet person to Person (I strongly sensed it was God speaking), I said, "I choose You." Everything has been different since that moment.

At that time I didn't know what word would describe Whom I had encountered: God, Creator, Ultimate Reality, Father, Holy Spirit, Jesus, The Source, The Real, or Life, as in the "I am Life." C.S. Lewis sometimes referred to God as "The Real" and there in Brightmoor Tabernacle such a name made sense. I had been shown that I was living in unreality, calling it reality. My entire perception had been flipped and reversed. With different eyes I watched the people singing and praying during the rest of the Sunday service. They were not religious nuts playing church and going through mechanical motions. I could see that they were in The Real and they knew it. They were *alive* with real life.

For years I had thought that God as a person was dead and, if there was a God, It was an impersonal Force coursing through the depths of everyone and everything. But what I was experiencing in this church was neither a return of the old, transcendent, out-there God, nor was it the awakening of my Higher Self merging with the ocean of Divinity that supposedly coursed through everything.

I did not obey the inner impulse I felt, but it was clearly there in me: to bow down to the Person who spoke to me and who was in this church and involved with these people. I was in the presence of an awesome Being. Yet this Being was personal and inviting.

In reflecting on this scene, I believe that the aroma of God's love that had drifted through my seemingly impenetrable defenses and touched me on Wednesday evening now manifested itself in full fragrance. On that Sunday I was in the presence of Love, and Love was clearly and unmistakably a Person.

Also, when I said "I choose You," it was my choice but in my guarded, critical, selfish little self, I don't think I was capable of so grand and life-changing a decision on my own. The Hound of Heaven had been tracking me and found me.

God's sovereignty and the gift of human choice are still mysterious to me, as to how they interweave in human lives. Something happened that day in Brightmoor Tabernacle, and it was clearly God's Favor setting the scene; and my response of *yes* to God's invitation was also part of the equation. Both Favor and human choice were factors, and a deed was done that day which would change my life forever.

Things Get Worse Before They Get Better

I cannot speak for what my fiancée was experiencing at that time, but after the Sunday at Brightmoor she joined me in taking a preparatory class for anyone inquiring about the Christian faith and for those intending to make a profession of faith. Although our conversion-stories were different, both of us recognized that the God we encountered in Brightmoor was the God of the Bible. Toward the end of 1984, prior to the completion of the course, we were married at a town hall by a Justice of the Peace (We had asked the pastor to marry us but he declined—we were seekers but not yet believers.). In February of 1985, we had finished the preparatory class and had accepted the Gospel of Jesus Christ. We were baptized, full-immersion style, in front of the whole congregation.

I felt hopeful but cautious at the same time. I had never really arrived at a landing place in my life. Had I finally come *home* or was this another transient stepping stone? Walking down into the baptismal font, I committed to jump into this new venture with all I had, following the choice I had made when I said "I choose You," but I didn't really know what I was stepping into and how it would turn out.

As mind-renewal began by reading the Word in the Bible and by listening to the preaching of the Word, an exchange-process began. Prior to our conversions, my wife and I had been involved in various New Age communities and had in our possession troves of quartz crystals, books on reincarnation and clairvoyance, occult paintings, New Age music, astrological charts, and other esoteric odds and ends. We had been advised that occult objects and books were tentacles of connection that needed to be severed, so we tossed and burned the objects. However, this change-out of external paraphernalia took years to complete, attached as we had become to much of it.

The inner change-out was even more difficult. Again, I can only speak for myself. We moved to North Carolina in 1986. As the tubes from my old life-support system were removed, my puffed-up, "divinized" self was exposed, along with the pain, fear, and anger that had been suppressed and numbed for many years. God had spoken to me that Sunday in Michigan. But when all the soul-gunk began oozing out to the surface, I became overwhelmed and didn't know where to turn. We began searching in North Carolina for a church in which to continue our journey.

We would go to a fundamentalist-type church but it would feel like the legalistic Catholic church of my youth. Fleeing this legalistic bad movie which I had seen before, we tried prophetic and charismatic congregations. I liked the freedom I found there but wasn't so sure about the "thus sayeth the Lord" prophecies, spoken between sips of coffee; and I wasn't so sure about whether the shouting, laughing, and body-gyrations were of the Holy Spirit. But I sought mentoring help wherever it might be found. This turned into a frantic search that involved many churches, pastors, Christian counselors, Bible studies, seminars, retreats, tapes, and books.

Basically I felt overwhelmed. My wife and I now had two sons, plus her three children from her previous marriage, plus regular vacation-visits from my son who was living with his mother in California. My unmedicated pain, anxiety, and anger came roiling out. I was surprised by the amount of repressed anger in me—anger at my wife, anger at my parents, anger at God, and anger at myself.

With all this pent-up anger and pain in me, and my wife's anger and pain coming into the picture as well, our marriage continued for a few more years until she asked for a separation in April of 1994. A divorce followed in 1997.

I did not walk out of this marriage as I had done in my previous marriages. Immature though I was in my Christian walk, I had changed enough to have a conviction that it was not right to run again. I wanted the marriage to be healed and restored, so I sought the counsel of pastors, counselors, and friends. In 1997 I wrote a last-gasp letter in which I proposed a process of reconciliation. Responding by letter, she declined.

I don't blame her for not wanting to continue in the marriage. My life was not surrendered to God enough for His power to be fully effective in my life. I discovered that trying harder to change *behavior* without changing out underlying bad *beliefs* was a recipe for exacerbating the problems. My ego was still in the driver's seat. The power of the Holy Spirit was growing within me but, at best, He was a co-pilot.

I deeply regret the pain and strife that I inflicted upon my former wives and our children. I continue to pray that God, as The Master Weaver, will work good for us all as we let Him weave the threads of our lives into the designs He has purposed for each of us in His loving heart.

From Humanistic Psychologist to Christian Counselor

In the middle of the decade between 1984 and 1994, a seismic shift of consciousness was set into motion—a paradigm-shift that affected me personally and professionally. As the numbing of my "life-support system" wore off, and as New Age spirituality lost its deceptive sheen, an inconvenient truth was about to emerge. While attending a church in Chapel Hill, North Carolina, at the direction of some men who were mentoring me, I fasted and prayed for over two weeks, consuming only fluids. Then I met with the men and they asked me what God had shown me. I began telling them the story of my life, and by the end of it experienced, through my own disclosure and their questions and comments, a striking conviction of the far-reaching depth of my self-centeredness and self-absorption.

It was like looking below the surface of a huge iceberg to encompass its true size, but what I saw was overwhelmingly massive. I broke down into tears for a long time, confronted so soberly by the pervasiveness of my pride, arrogance, and sense of entitlement. I cringed at what I saw of critical, judgmental, prejudicial streaks in my soul.

I felt helpless. In that moment, like none before, I knew that I needed a Savior. The name *Jesus* made full and complete sense to me, beyond what I had experienced in Michigan. I now knew who Jesus was at a deeper level than before. My relationship with Him broadened as I thanked Him, in the presence of the men, for all He had done.

As a humanistic psychologist, I had thrown out the word *sin* along with my old theology books. As a New Ager I had cleverly disguised evil as ignorance. But in that moment with those men, and in many moments following that event, I had an experiential sense of the reality of sin and evil.

After moving to North Carolina, I first worked in a mental health center and then in a smoking cessation clinic, but gradually shifted toward the spiritual understanding of healing. I began networking in

Christian counseling circles, meeting many Christian counselors and pastors in the area, and even began to see patients privately in a home-office. I read voraciously, listened to tapes, and attended seminars. Finally I landed a job in a Christian counseling center in Cary.

What I encountered in the field of Christian counseling was basically the same cognitive therapy of my secular training in psychotherapy. Secular therapy focused on positive thoughts of succeeding, winning, and learning to adapt. Christian counseling added in thoughts from the Bible that focused on God's goodness, provision, and love.

The Scriptures were rich and deep, such as "Be transformed by the renewing of your mind" (Romans 12:2), and "...it is no longer I who live but Christ lives in me" (Galatians 2:20), suggesting significant and thorough change. However, for the most part, the therapeutic approach of Christian counseling focused almost solely on *immediate consciousness*, the top layer of the mind. The hidden issues in the heart were barely addressed.

From God's Word it seemed abundantly clear to me that the darkened depths of human nature were extensive (and I had discovered this to be true in my own life) and that all humans have hidden anxieties which need to be searched out. Yet most of what I learned and tried to apply in Christian counseling were concepts, principles, applications, and coping strategies...all in the form of the counselor downloading Bible verses and advice from his or her mind into the mind of the client.

The rationale seemed to be that if clients, indeed all Christians, could push the right thoughts into their minds, the power of these holy thoughts would shove the negative, false, sinful thoughts out.[1] Strategies that I witnessed (and used on myself and on others) included repetition, exhortation, inundation, shouting, denouncing, and rebuking. Counselor advice might include repeating Bible verses over and over for a month, or putting these verses on 5"x7" cards on a

---

[1] I do not discount the power of the Holy Spirit in the Word to penetrate deeply. I will discuss later in the book.

bathroom mirror as constant reminders—trying to pound in the new knowledge. I heard pastors shouting out phrases such as "God loves you!" from the pulpit, as though the force of an elevated decibel level might drive the truth below the surface waters of the mind.

We Christian counselors would enlist the blessings of the Holy Spirit at the beginning of the session and then relegate Him to the role of a silent bystander and witness. At the end of the session we would call on Him to close the meeting. I fell into this same pattern even though I knew with my head-knowledge that the Holy Spirit was called Counselor, Healer, Comforter, and the Light who searches darkened regions of hearts to show truthfully what is going on there. And, further, I knew that He is a Person who can communicate with us in any moment. We were not tapping into the Holy Spirit as the primary source of healing.

Similar to secular therapy, there was an implicit belief that if a person could only grasp the correct knowledge in his or her mind, then healing would happen. This is like receiving a diagnosis of having a malignant tumor and believing that a cure will now magically happen because you correctly understand the problem, and you understand what is needed to correct the problem. You have to remove the tumor.

Some change and healing occurred in me and in my patients but it was more symptom-reduction than real healing; more managing and coping than root-healing that brought peace; more tentative improvement and adjustment to circumstances than actual transformation. I didn't realize it at the time but what was missing was the action of *replacing old thought-patterns that were embedded in regions of the mind deeper than immediate consciousness.* What would become clear later is the necessity to *remove* and *replace* dysfunctional beliefs, not try to shove them aside.

Up to this point, in the early 1990s, I had neither the understanding nor the skill to remove old interpretations and beliefs. I didn't realize it but *soul-surgery* was needed, not palliative care. But I had not yet met a Christian counselor or pastor who had expertise in spiritual-surgery.

The truth was right there but I didn't see it: Didn't Jesus remove the old and replace it with the new? He did not shove anything aside, He replaced it, He made it new—a new creation. Wasn't the mission of

Jesus to substitute, to replace, to exchange at the deepest levels of our being? Didn't Jesus tell us that the Holy Spirit would be directly involved in showing us all truth? Those questions did not occur to me then.

Desperate Times Call for Desperate Measures

In summary, I became more and more committed in my relationship with the Lord Jesus but I still had a very troubled heart. I was separated from my wife and children, and the deep arrows of separation-anxiety and rejection from earlier years of my life were still in place—the pain of which was exacerbated by my current situation. The failure and upheaval in my family was painfully felt anew each time I had to return my sons, Adrian and John, to Chapel Hill after a visit, or take my first-born son, Adam, to the airport. I was distraught most of the time.

Out of painful desperation I called out to God and appealed to Him to do something *real* in me, in my life-situation, and in this whole ministry of counseling to which I felt more and more called. I had not yet found effective healing for myself or my patients but I hoped for more, and now I desperately pleaded for more. That prayer would be answered soon enough.

Chapter 4

Real Healing

In 1993, my private practice as a full-time Christian counselor began in a basement office given to me by the Fellowship of Christ Church in the town of Cary, North Carolina. My counseling style focused on trying to implant biblically based thoughts about how God sees us, hoping that these thoughts would override self-defeating thoughts that kept people chained to negative emotions and unwanted behavior. I was practicing the Christian cognitive therapy that I spoke of in the last chapter.

As a counselor I thought it my job to be a storehouse of appropriate Bible verses, stress management strategies, addiction-breaking secrets, and other information that I could download into my patients' minds to make them well. Some of my patients knew the Bible better than I did but they were hoping I could help them move the truth that they knew in their heads to their hearts and then into their behavior.

The shared understanding among my colleagues was that there was an invisible barrier between head and heart that needed to be penetrated in some way. Hence the aforementioned methods of taping Bible verses onto the bathroom mirror and listening to sermons over and over on audio tapes. It was generally accepted in my profession that our main problems were in the hidden regions of the heart, but the struggle was how to get in there.

Up to this point, I had not really seen patients healed (restored to a state of true wellbeing) either by secular or by faith-based counseling. Mostly I had seen temporary alleviation of symptoms, which would eventually return. Patients could learn to cope with and adjust to their situations, cobbling together strategies and advice for reducing stress and conflict. They learned to toughen up and survive trauma. With counseling advice they could cut back on addictive substances or behaviors. Sometimes patients even mustered the willpower to quit an addiction...similar to a person going off a pain medication.

But the emotional pain persisted. *Real healing* was rare. There seemed to be blocks and resistances that stayed in place—no matter the amount of truth-thoughts heaped on to try to move things along.

And then, in 1995, along came Nancy.

The Light Shines into the Darkness

The woman walked slowly into my office and slumped down into a chair, her first statement a heavy sigh. Nancy was a pleasant-looking woman in her mid-forties, but her complexion was pale and there was deep weariness in her eyes and shoulders. I wondered how long she had been so burdened, months certainly, maybe years. Her husband, Tom, came in behind her and took a chair slightly off to the side. He had a quiet demeanor and looked at his wife as though he were her bodyguard. The focus was clearly on her.

Nancy began her story by recounting an event that had happened eight months previously, while driving to meet a client. She was an interior decorator, working in the Raleigh, NC area for the past several years. Suddenly, without warning, she felt grabbed by a panic attack: intense fear, pounding heart, shaking, shortness of breath, and sweating. There was also dizziness and fear that she was going crazy or even dying. She pulled off the road shortly after the attack began and when it passed she caught her breath and returned to work, though badly shaken by the event.

Nancy shifted nervously in her chair as she proceeded to tell me that several more panic attacks occurred over the next six weeks. She would have fear of having an attack, and that would bring on another attack. She also had intermittent anxiety unrelated to anything except the anticipation of having another panic attack. In short, she began to fit the criteria described for Panic Disorder in the *Diagnostic and Statistical Manual of Mental Disorders*.

The weariness I saw in her eyes and body language was from fighting fear. She was worn out from the struggle and was just waiting for the next time the claws of fear would jump out of nowhere and grab her again. She was still having occasional panic attacks.

During the weeks after the first panic attack, Nancy had sought help from a psychiatrist and a psychotherapist, and she told me about the two medications she was currently taking. The medications had slowed down the frequency of the attacks, but the undercurrent of anxiety was almost continually present. The psychotherapy did not seem to be helping. She had heard about me from a friend who had come to see me for therapy. Nancy said she did not know if her problem had any spiritual basis, but she was a Christian and wanted a Christian counselor. She added that she was very desperate and knew she needed God's power to get through what had become the crisis of her life.

She had quit her job and had become a recluse, sitting at home with the blinds closed. She could not drive anymore. Her husband, an avid fisherman, enjoyed going to the coast on fishing trips. However, she could not tolerate her husband being more than 50 miles away without having a wave of anxiety. She said she felt sad that he couldn't go any more. Her husband spoke up to say that he was willingly sacrificing his hobby; he just wanted her to get well. Though they did not say so, I guessed this crisis was a strain on their marriage. There was heaviness in the air.

Both Nancy and Tom were carrying heavy burdens and had showed up at my doorstep for help. What could I offer that would be effective and healing? An alleviation of symptoms would not do here, and I began to feel a burden myself. For some time I had thought that fear was, at the root, a spiritual problem and so I agreed to walk into that darkness with them. It was a big problem, I said, but added that "Nothing is too big for God." I could hear the uncertainty in my voice and wondered if they could hear it as well. Evidently those were the words she wanted to hear. She smiled weakly and said she would like to begin treatment with me. We set an appointment for the following week. Slowly they got up from their chairs and we said good-bye.

On the day of her next appointment, Nancy returned to my office looking about the same as she had the week before. I turned from my desk and rolled my chair around to face her. Her husband once again sat off to the side, watching.

I began by asking Nancy to start telling the story of her life, from the very beginning. In my practice, I used autobiography as a primary way to dig below the surface into the deeper issues of one's life. I clarified for Nancy that I was not asking her to give me background information. Rather, I was asking her to tell her life-story, year by year, chapter by chapter. We would listen together and try to hear the underlying themes, motifs, recurrent threads...bringing the story right up to the present day.

Nancy began describing a chaotic beginning with an early breakup between her mother and father. After Nancy's father exited, she lived with her mother, whom she described as having a serious alcohol problem coupled with significant mental health issues. She recounted an early memory at age four, in which she was standing outside the front door of a house, suitcase by her side, watching her mother walk away and then drive off. Her mother was evidently unable to cope with her problems and also raise Nancy, so she gave her away to her childless sister and brother-in-law who lived in another town.

Nancy then described the ranch-style house of her aunt and uncle. Their bedroom was at one end of the house and Nancy's at the other end. I asked her to describe what life was like living with them in their home. She said they were strict and not warm folks. As an example, she told of having to sleep in her bedroom without having any light, even from the bathroom nearby. Plead though Nancy often did, her aunt and uncle would not relent.

She said, "I have memories of being in my bed, covers pulled up to my chin, just scared to death." At this point in the session, she closed her eyes without any direction from me, perhaps because the memory was so strong and vivid.

I asked, "Were you alone there?" "Yes," she said. "My aunt and uncle were either in the living room or had gone to bed. I didn't know which because they always closed my door."

What happened next will sound odd to your ears, as it did to mine. "Who else was there?" I asked. I immediately felt foolish. Nancy had just told me she was alone. Why did I ask such a dumb question? At that time in my life I had few spiritual thoughts about God's omnipresence and that He would be there; I was not fishing for that response.

"No one, I was alone."

My self-talk was, "Move on, Bill, she said she was alone and feeling very afraid."

I was about to push on into having her describe more of her life in that home, when, still with eyes closed, she said, "Oh...God was there!" Her face brightened as she was seeing something happen in the memory. "The whole room is filled with light and Jesus is standing next to my bed. I know it is Him." Moments passed. "He is touching my arm and telling me that He loves me and that He will always be with me to take care of me."

We stayed in that memory for a while, both of us soaking in what was happening. "All the fear is gone," she finally said. "All the fear is gone and I just feel so peaceful."

I looked over at Tom. He was also absorbing what was taking place. No longer watching from the sideline, he looked to be very engaged and drawn into what was occurring, though a startled look was also evident in his eyes.

I did not know what to do next. Nancy opened her eyes and began to weep copious tears of relief and joy. It was as though the person before me had been released from a dark dungeon. She was overcome with the emotion of gaining freedom after long years of living in the grip of fear. Her tears were those of release and of freedom. Coming out of my own absorption in this scene, my mind slowly cleared. I focused and then like the sharp peal of a bell going off in my brain, I astutely knew what to do next...I handed Nancy a box of Kleenex. That was easily the most significant contribution I made to the proceedings that day.

We debriefed for a while then drew the session to a close and set up another appointment for the following week. Nancy and Tom had much to absorb, as did I. Somehow I knew that things would never be the same for them and things would never be the same for me. Real healing had begun for her, and real training had begun for me.

Healing and Training Continue

When Nancy and Tom returned the following week, I began by asking her how she was doing. Although a habituated heaviness and weariness were still present in much of her body language, there was light in her eyes and new energy in her voice. She first said that the memory of being alone at night in the darkened bedroom had changed. She still had a sense of Jesus' presence there and the room was filled with light. Several times she had tried in her mind to make the bedroom dark again, but she could not. And, she added, the fear was still completely gone. The three of us exchanged words of amazement and then resumed the process of Nancy telling her life-story.

As you might imagine, Nancy had lots of anxiety and fear growing up. Rejection and abandonment created a sense of isolation, and she always felt on the outside looking in. Her sense of self-confidence and self-worth were very low, and she found her way into peer groups in which the members also saw themselves as outsiders. She had not gone off the deep end into drugs and promiscuity, but in her younger years, she found alcohol and food to be useful pain relievers and comforters. She and her husband had joined a church. Both of them became involved in church activities and services, but she always felt an emotional distance from God. She tried to please Him by behaving well, though when she failed she always felt anxious and guilty for having disappointed Him.

During the next six weeks of treatment, unusual and unprecedented healing occurred. Nancy did not again have a visual manifestation of Jesus in her memories, but a felt-sense of His Presence seeped into her memories as she continued telling her story. It was as though His Presence flashed through her whole life from the initial blast of Light in the bedroom memory. She would be describing a scene in adolescence, for example, talking about how lonely and dejected she felt...and then she would interject, "Oh, but Jesus was there." She would pause for a few moments, letting that thought enter the memory, and the feelings in the memory would change from negative to positive.

I did not pull out my 3x5 cards and write Scripture verses for her to read and repeat. She simply let the Presence of the Lord come into each event in her life as she recounted it. He dissolved the anxiety, boosted her fragile self-image, and removed the doubts about her prospects for the future. I was watching someone come alive before my eyes as we progressed year by year, chapter by chapter, up to the present.

She experienced *being with* rather than *being alone*, *being loved* in place of *being rejected*, and *being valuable* instead of *being outcast*. It was a changing-out, an exchanged-life process that was actual, not merely conceptual. There was no therapeutic task of getting truth or positive thoughts from her head to her heart. As I saw it, she had opened her simple faith to acknowledge the truth that God was in that bedroom with her. He walked right in through the opening of her faith and, from there, He entered any soul-room (memory) in which she came to the door and said, "Come in."

As the weeks went by and I listened to her, I often thought of the passage in Revelation 3:20 NIV: "Here I am! I stand at the door and knock. If anyone hears My voice and opens the door, I will come in to him and eat with him, and he with Me." Nancy heard Jesus' voice, kept opening doors for Him to come in, and eagerly savored the delicious meal of His Presence.

I had always liked that verse from the Book of Revelation, but now the passage came alive for me as well as for Nancy. I experienced the Lord calling me to open the door of my life. I knew that I wanted to let Him in, but I had little idea what it would mean for Him to *eat* with me and I with Him. I would learn that soon enough.

Within three months Nancy had discontinued all of her medications without any severe withdrawal symptoms. She had no more panic attacks. She returned to her work, driving there herself. The last time she came to my office, she came without her husband. She looked like a different person. Gone were the weary look, the forlorn voice, the shuffling gait. She was full of life and energy, and light beamed from her eyes. At the end of the session we agreed that she would call me on an as-needed basis. As she went through the doorway of my office, she turned around and said, "Tom has gone back to his fishing at the coast." She smiled, turned and left. I smiled at the thought of Tom out there fishing, enjoying his freedom in the surf and the wind.

The Rest of the Story

I never saw Nancy or Tom again, but I did receive a phone call from Nancy about eight years later. They had moved out of state, but she had been in touch with a friend in our area who was experiencing emotional difficulties. She said that she wanted to refer her friend to see me and wondered if I was taking new patients. "But," she said, "before we talk about that, Dr. Day, I want to tell you something." She paused, and then emphatically said, "I'm still healed!"

She updated me on her life: She had never had another panic attack, and her life kept getting better in many ways. She then said again, "I'm healed."

Nancy concluded her update by telling me that she was now in ministry as a speaker for women's conferences and retreats within her denomination. I asked her what she spoke on. She said, "I just tell my life-story, how Perfect Love casts out fear."

In the moment she said that last sentence, I had a shaft of light penetrate my understanding with the wondrous ways of God. He had allowed all those miserable experiences to happen in Nancy's life, experiences in which fear and loneliness seemingly ate up her time and energy. Yet He knew that one day, in His sovereign timing, when she turned her heart and her whole life over to Him, chapter by chapter, He would transform and enliven her...and enrich the lives of others through her.

The First Epistle of John 4:18 says, "...perfect love casts out fear." That portion of Scripture was no longer just words on a page, it was living in her. She was a witness to that truth, and her life now had a purpose beyond herself: to share this truth with others. She ended her phone call by saying how fulfilling it was to be right in the center of God's purpose for her.

In 1995, at the bottom of her pit of fear, Nancy had desperately prayed for healing. Her prayer had been answered far beyond what she had imagined possible. From the depths of despair to the heights of ministering to women about the power of Love, she was securely in the hands of God like a bow and arrow in the hands of an archer.

In 2003, when I received the phone call from Nancy, I was finally becoming immersed in inner healing ministry. But in 1995, instead of jumping into this stream of healing that God was showing me through Nancy's healing, I stayed ankle-deep in it. I began to read books on inner healing but mostly I remained a cognitive Christian counselor, sitting in the driver's seat of therapy sessions.

In my "training session" with Nancy, the Holy Spirit had shifted me into the role of an assistant and facilitator, but I did not stay in that role for patients who came after Nancy. Rather than directly appealing to the Holy Spirit and trusting His guidance, occasionally I would suggest to patients that God had been with them in the dark, lonely places in their lives...and sometimes breakthroughs in healing would occur with this approach. However, when there was any resistance to my suggestion, or when patients did not see, hear, or sense God's presence, I had no clue as to what to do next. Slowly I slipped back into my counselor role and continued to dole out advice.

Real Healing for Me

In my personal life, some healing had begun in me as I read the Word and absorbed truth through counseling and pastoral care. But something vital was missing. My sense of *belonging* was experientially threadbare and I didn't understand why. In church after church, sermon after sermon, book after book, I heard the repeated message that God was a Father who loved me, forgave me, and now accepted me as His son. But I had the same problem I witnessed in many of my patients, especially the men: I *knew* of God's love and acceptance in my head, but I didn't really believe or *experience* His love in my heart.

About one year after the conclusion of Nancy's therapy, the parable of the talents kept coming to my attention in sermons and Scripture readings. The end of the parable reads: "...And cast the unprofitable servant into the outer darkness. There will be weeping and gnashing of teeth" (Matthew 25:30). Every time I read or heard that passage I felt a niggling discomfort and would quickly turn my attention away from it.

One day, while sitting at my desk, I ran across the parable yet again and felt the same discomfort. This time I spoke inwardly to the Lord: "Lord, please show me the truth about what I am feeling." This time I did not divert my attention away from the emotion. Immediately what appeared out of that murky feeling was a realization, a belief, that *I was that man in the outer darkness*. Then it was no longer a niggling discomfort I felt, it was fear.

I stayed with the experience, asking the Holy Spirit to guide me. I inquired as to why I was in the outer darkness, and a deeper belief came forward into my conscious mind: I believed that *I belonged in the outer darkness because the amount of sin and evil I had done in the 20 years of my wayward living was too much to be fully forgiven.*

I was stunned by this revelation and immediately challenged it with the truths I had read in the Bible and had learned during the past 10 years: In Jesus I was fully forgiven; He died for all my sins, past, present, and future; His Atonement means I have been reconciled with God and restored to fellowship with Him.

In the weeks that followed, I became painfully aware that I could not exchange my inner beliefs with the truths I cognitively knew. The "wall" between my head and my heart was firmly in place. Through coaching and guidance from a pastor-friend, I realized two things: (1) these beliefs were deeply entrenched remnants of beliefs from my Catholic upbringing, and (2) my own performance-driven striving would be futile to resolve the issue.

During these weeks, memories came of my mother telling me to "be a good boy, Billy," just about every time I left the house as a child. Other memories came, of catechism lessons about God's expectation that I could be good if I tried hard enough, with some help from Him of course.

The struggle inside grew, inner turmoil and agitation grew, and I became increasingly desperate. I discovered verses in Ezekiel 36:

> I will sprinkle clean water on you, and you will be clean; I will cleanse you from all your impurities and from all your idols. I

will give you a new heart and put a new spirit within you; I will remove from you your heart of stone and give you a heart of flesh. And I will put My Spirit in you and move you to follow My decrees and be careful to keep my laws (Ezekiel 36:25-27 NIV).

Upon waking each morning, I would pray through the verses—with my heart, soul, mind, and strength. My prayer became a simple, desperate plea: for God to break open my hardened heart and replace it with a heart into which He would pour His Spirit.

Breakthrough

This went on for many weeks. Like the persistent friend who comes at midnight (Lk.11:5-9) I kept knocking and asking. I was calling out to God with everything I had. Then one day it happened. I was alone at home, lying prostrate on the floor, crying out to God. I had my Bible with me down on the floor. In my mind's eye I saw the word *Galatians.* I opened to that epistle and felt inwardly directed to go to Chapter 4, not knowing what I would find there.

I began reading. When my eyes arrived at verse 7, "You are no longer a slave but a son..." that same personal Presence was speaking directly to me again. It was the Presence that I had previously experienced when I sought to know the truth about the inspiration of the Bible. Father God was present in that verse from Galatians, telling me that I was His son. Something in my heart broke, shattered, released. Then there was a softening...and I felt love, life, and peace flow into my heart.

The lie that *I belonged in the outer darkness* was blown away by the powerful truth that I was accepted as a son and belonged in the Kingdom. In that moment I was in God's presence and I experienced being loved, father to son. The darkness of fear dissipated. The relief was incredible. I wept tears of great joy. I read the next verse, "...and if a son, then an heir of God through Christ," and felt the truth of Jesus saying that He had come to set captives free (Luke 4). I felt free, I felt safe, and sensations of coming alive swept into my soul. I looked at verse 6, "And because you are sons, God has sent forth the Spirit of His

Son into your hearts, crying out, 'Abba, Father!'" I experienced that truth in my heart. It was a new heart, as depicted in those verses of Ezekiel. God had removed my heart of stone and had given me a heart of flesh, into which he was pouring His Spirit.

It was new and it was uncanny but I eagerly accepted what was happening. I spoke words out loud, for the first time experiencing their truth for me: "Father, Abba, Daddy." More tears of joy and relief. I *belonged*. I was on the inside, no longer on the outside. I savored the peace that came with this realization. This was a peace that would gradually grow, from that moment until today, as I continue growing into my true identity as a son of the King, living in His Kingdom.

Since that moment I have been living in the best part of the prodigal son story, the part where the father comes running out to meet his miserably unhappy son, embracing him with outstretched arms, and saying to him with all his father's love, "welcome home, my son."

Over the next weeks, I turned to Galatians 4:7 frequently to hear God whisper those words of truth and love. Tucked away inside of me were more lies and false interpretations of life-experiences that would have to be changed out. However, this breakthrough was a beginning. It was a replacement "ritual" for the dedication-ritual prayed over me when I was two weeks old. For more than 50 years I had lived first with a priest-identity, then with no identity at all. Now I knew in my head, in my heart, and in my spirit, that I was a *beloved son.*

Building on my aforementioned conversion-experience, this experience was a major event in my soul deepening its relationship with God; it was also a major therapeutic intervention in the treatment of my anxiety disorder. True heart-healing had begun. My conversion experience in Brightmoor Tabernacle had been a true beginning in many ways, but this current event felt (and still does) as though it was the first day of my life. It was the day I came to experience that I was a beloved son and that I had a Father to whom I belonged. I was His. And I knew that He had intentions and purposes for me. He was calling me to participate in His Kingdom. I felt connected and *attached* at the core of my being, something I had never felt before.

A truth settled into my heart-knowledge: that the *Life* of "I am Life" is relational in nature. As a son, in relationship to God my Father, I felt alive. The sense of attachment and belonging was the deepest that I had ever experienced. It was like coming home . . . for the first time.

Inner Healing 101: Basic Training Classes

I began to note the steps of the healing process, realizing that I was not only being healed but also trained for what God had in mind for me. I saw similarities between my healing and Nancy's. Here are some gleanings.

1. I saw that the substance of the "wall" which I thought existed between head and heart was actually a lie buried in my mind. Somehow I had formed a belief which was contrary to the biblical truth that God has forgiven all my sins in Christ Jesus. I believed that I had gone *over the limit* in sinning and couldn't be fully forgiven. Below the surface of my immediate consciousness, my mind had formed the understanding that my destiny was to be in the outer darkness. Amazingly, this belief had the power to serve as a deflective shield, turning away thoughts of God's full forgiveness. The lie: *I had not been fully forgiven* was hidden somewhere in the folds of my mind. Discovering that lie was like finding a secret dungeon in which a part of me was living in darkness, literally feeling like an outcast. God revealed that lie when I asked Him to show me what was going on.

    For many years, below the surface of Nancy's immediate consciousness, Nancy had carried around bleak memories of being alone and abandoned at an early age. When God shone the light of His Presence into those memories, the belief: *that she had been abandoned* was replaced by the truth of *God-there-with-her*, taking care of her. This new understanding had a transformative effect on how she saw God, herself, and herself in relation to others.

    A keen interest began to form in me about learning how to access these hidden regions. What was being appropriately dismantled in my understanding was the mistaken notion that the arena for renewal and healing (as in "the renewing of your mind" in Rom. 2:12) was in the immediately-conscious part of my mind. There were more layers to the mind than the top layer.

2. Another awareness that broke through was that in any given moment my full will is not totally available to make whole-hearted decisions. Part of being double-minded can be that I have a divided will. Since my profession of faith in 1985, I had been in churches in which it was expected that, with the impartation of the Holy Spirit and the huge body of knowledge in Christian doctrine, a person *should* be transformed in spirit, heart, mind, and behavior. More than once I had heard sermons and counsel about how we should be able to "get over it" or "put it behind you," referring to old beliefs, doubts, and behavior.

   Both Nancy and I had stuffed our heads with truths that contradicted the lies we held in our hearts, but these embedded beliefs had been there for years and had formidable override-power. I gave a 100% effort to will God's love down into that place, but I didn't have 100% of my will available to me. Unbeknown to me, part of my will was locked into the belief that I was unforgiven. The Holy Spirit showed me that lie. Then His truth, spoken right into the face of the lie, had the power to break its hold, as I gladly *chose* to receive His truth in place of the lie.

   The key insight regarding the *will* was that the interpretations, beliefs, and conclusions that I had come to were not purely cognitive in nature. It was apparent that willpower was embedded within these interpretations. I had somewhere, somehow *decided* that God wouldn't forgive me. I had *decided* that I was unforgiven. Nancy had *decided* that God had abandoned her. When *I released* that decision in order to receive God's truth in Gal. 4:7, my will became aligned with His will.

3. Finally, in both cases, Nancy's and mine, healing and trans-formation happened through the direct intervention of God. He showed up through dialogue and personal involvement, not indirectly through an application of propositions and principles. It was the personal engagement of God that fostered healing, not human-centered counseling.

In Ezekiel 36:25:27 God does every action: cleansing, giving a new heart, putting in a new spirit, removing the heart of stone, giving a heart of flesh into which He puts His Spirit, who then moves the person to keep God's laws. I had experienced the truth of this Scripture: that God had done it all by His power. My *co-laboring* consisted of: asking, praying, seeking for truth, being persistent, calling out with everything in me because I was desperate, ceasing from trying to do anything to fix the problem myself, and putting my trust and hope in the Lord.

In Nancy's encounters with the Lord, she had no doubt that, from start to finish, God had cast out her fear and given her peace.

Several months after my healing time with the Lord, a patient came to see me who would confirm these insights and deepen my understanding of inner healing.

Chapter 5

Matters of Life and Death

The Right to Life: Mary's Story

Mary was a believer, in her 30s, married, with two children. She had come to me seeking help for anxiety about many things in her life. Whenever a sign of sickness would occur she would quickly become convinced that she had cancer or some other life-threatening disease. She had become an expert in every known herbal supplement, and when she first came to see me she was going to a naturopath for weekly "detoxification" treatments. She had perfectionist tendencies and felt that she was falling short of being a good wife and mother.

Whenever she had these feelings her anxiety level would ramp up considerably. The emotions would quickly enter a theological arena: she would express beliefs that God was disappointed in her and that her health problems were probably punishment for her poor performance in life. When Mary came for therapy she was weary of being on an anxiety roller-coaster. Recently she had gone through another cycle of fear about her health, which had been dispelled by a medical test that showed normalcy.

After several sessions of anxiety management Mary began sharing at a deeper level. One day she told me of a memory of when she was nine years old. Her parents were arguing in the living room. Mary was out of sight in the hallway listening. In the course of the argument she heard her mother bitterly remind her husband how, when she was pregnant with Mary, she had unsuccessfully tried to abort her. As Mary described this memory she was seized by the emotion that was still contained in the memory, and she closed her eyes and stopped talking.

I asked, "What is going on inside that girl after she heard those words?"

There was a long silence. Then she said, "I was supposed to die. I'm not supposed to be alive." She opened her eyes, startled at this inner revelation.

I engaged Mary in dialogue about the nature and implications of this realization. We had located a hidden belief, planted there many years ago: *that she did not have a legitimate right to live.* If everything had gone according to plan, her life would have been terminated. Could it be that this belief had spread out into her life all these years like ripples in a pond spreading outward from a dropped stone? From experiencing the power of my buried belief about over-the-limit sinning, I thought it possible.

In a subsequent session Mary and I discussed her hypochondria and her perfectionist tendencies as evidence that something in her was in agreement with this belief about not having a right to live. The hypochondria caused her to fear an early death; the perfectionism pushed her to "earn a right to live" by flawless performance. In one of our discussions, Psalm 139 came to mind. I read the following passage to her:

> For You have formed my inward parts; you have knit me together in my mother's womb. I will praise You, for I am fearfully and wonderfully made....How precious also are Your thoughts to me, O God" (v. 13,14,17).

I tried to refute the lie by telling her God's truth: He created her and He wanted her to live. He had given to her the right to life. She responded that she knew this was true. Our dialogue did not dislodge the lie. I was still a novice, not fully an apprentice in the Potter's Hands. I was still exerting human effort to try to fix the problem.

Not much happened. Mary realized some relief of her symptoms as a light of understanding illumined the roots of the problem. We tried a couple of times to invite the Lord into the memory but this did not bear fruit. In the course of our discussions I told her about how I had engaged with the Lord by praying through passages of Ezekiel 36—God replacing my heart of stone. Mary's lie of not having a right to live seemed as stonily entrenched as my lie had been. Mary listened and said she would give that a try with Psalm 139.

More than a month went by. One day Mary came in with radiance in her countenance I had not seen before. She told me that every day for the past month she had been praying through Psalm 139, putting herself in the verses in place of the Psalmist David. She described a process whereby she began dialoguing with the Lord in a more intimate way than ever before. And one day He was present to her in the words of the Psalm, speaking directly to her: "Mary, I formed your inward parts. I knit you together in your mother's womb...All My thoughts about you are precious to Me. You are precious to me. I have given you the right to live, for you are Mine."

The verses of Psalm 139 had pointed Mary to a dialogue with God. She accepted the invitation to engage with the Holy Spirit directly. Finally, after continued asking, seeking, and knocking, the power of the Holy Spirit broke through with healing words of truth. Mary had opened to Him the place of the lie. And when the Word Himself spoke into that place, she received Him and let Him replace the lie with His Truth. The Light obliterated the darkness.

As Mary spoke, I could see that the radiance in her was this Light of Truth rippling out from her soul. Deep within herself she now knew that she was a beloved daughter. She belonged to Him who is Life— who had given her life and the *right to life.* There was a wonderful peace and rest in her eyes. As the weeks went by we let the Lord's truth make its way through some habitual thought patterns of defeat, but mostly it was a simple mop-up operation. Mary told me laughingly that she had tried, but was unable, to make the old, impending-death beliefs return.

We stayed in touch by phone for awhile but the healing held. She was on a clear, new path, able to live more freely than ever before. I spoke with her by phone several years later. She and her family had moved to the Midwest. She was doing well and spoke of a ministry she was in with other women. She said that God was using her own healing to minister to women who were pregnant and trying to decide between abortion and adoption.

The End of an Era

Up to this point in my life I had never encountered any real enemies who opposed me or tried to hurt me in some way. But I now had a person in my private practice who was intent on discrediting me. It was a first-ever charge and it was false, but I was under investigation by my licensing board, and the whole stressful situation was generating much anxiety.

I sought out friends and colleagues for support and also for accountability as to what God was doing in this upheaval. My pastor, my brother, and a few close friends were especially helpful in the process of inviting and allowing the Lord to speak into my soul to reveal the places where I did not yet fully trust Him. There was still evidence of Bill-in-a-bubble (my childhood nightmares) acting autonomously.

What came to light, apart from my career crisis, was the realization that I had not yet fully surrendered the driver's seat of my life to the Lord. I was still making decisions by myself and subsequently checking with God for His blessing, rather than checking with Him before I made important decisions...similar to an employee going forward on a project without taking the plan to his boss first.

There was self-deception in that I didn't realize I was still engaged in this habitual way of acting. In His love, God brought it out into the open. Various situations in my life were beyond what I could control or manage and my self-sufficiency shriveled and shook, revealing its true impotence. But I did not fully trust that God was in control and that He would take care of me. In the circumstances of my life He was now kicking out the remaining blocks of self-sufficiency that had been in place for a long time, and I felt the shakiness of my trust in Him.

February 19, 1999 was the birthday of my youngest son, John, who was in France on a school-related trip, together with my second son, Adrian. The atmosphere in my apartment was anything but festive as the evening hours ushered in an inner darkness along with the usual darkness of nightfall. Earlier in the day, while walking across the parking lot to my car, I had felt an eerie sensation that I was actually in the biblical valley of the shadow of death of Psalm 23. I felt fear on that walk until I began reciting the verses of the Psalm, "I will fear no evil;

for You are with me....You prepare a table before me in the presence of my enemies." I felt temporary comfort.

It was close to midnight and, in my mind, it didn't seem that I could call anyone who could really help me. Something dark, fearful, and threatening congealed into an encompassing mass in my soul. I can't rationally or logically explain it other than to say that all of a sudden, I was in the middle of a tightening darkness.

I was past the time in my life when I might use drugs, alcohol, or sex to mitigate pain and fear. I felt trapped, with seemingly no way out. God seemed strangely absent. I felt more painfully alone than ever before and there didn't seem to be any hope at all for the future. I couldn't see how to go forward, and every way I thought of to get out from under the crushing weight felt fruitless and dead-ended.

Next, I saw myself, in my mind's eye, going to the kitchen, getting a knife, and killing myself. This seemed the only way out and there was a strong impulse in me to carry out what I saw in my mind. This had never happened to me before and I began to be afraid. The fear grew stronger because the impulse was not weakening. I was lying in my bed, trembling with fear, and my heart was beating wildly; it was so strong that I thought it was going to jump out of my chest. Out of total desperation, I began to call out, "Jesus...Jesus!" I felt nothing but the fullness of fear. I called out Jesus' name over and over, louder and louder, through tears and pain and increasing desperation, hour after hour...adding other phrases, like "Jesus have mercy on me." I was pleading for my life, still feeling nothing but the presence of death, darkness, and fear encircling me.

Then it happened. Just as the first rays of dawn came through the window, Jesus was there by the window near the faint rays of the dawn...a brilliant, radiating light in human shape. I was totally startled, but I knew it was Him. The visual Presence disappeared after a few moments and He was inside and all around me, speaking names to identify Himself: "Lord," "Savior," "Brother," "Friend," "Jesus."

I felt immense power surging through me, and His voice calming and comforting me. Very slowly I began to relax my muscles for the first time since the ordeal began hours ago. I was now clearly and safely in the arms of a very loving Presence and I gradually came to rest, amazed at what was happening...but fully welcoming it.

He began speaking words of comfort and truth into my understanding: I could go on in life; I didn't need to end things; He had plans for a good future for me. Also, I didn't have to go on alone; He would be with me and would not leave me. The fear ebbed away. All suicidal impulses vanished, and a deep peace began to settle in. Then a very curious thing happened: an invitation was extended to me to become more deeply connected with Him. The scene was almost like a wedding ceremony at an altar and I was being asked if I would accept this invitation. I said out loud that I would. Images began to blur, a deep tiredness and weariness seeped into the feeling of peace, and I fell asleep.

I awoke about five hours later feeling refreshed, with no traces of the awfulness from the previous night. But all I could think of was that I needed to go out and buy a ring. I didn't fully know why. Maybe it was to commemorate the event of last night? I dressed and went shopping for a ring, not knowing what I was looking for, but feeling guided. I didn't have the visual sight of Jesus or His voice from the previous night, but I knew He was with me.

In the third store I found a ring in a showcase. I immediately knew it was *the* ring. It had three small diamonds slanting across the band, and on either side of the diamonds were vine-like engravings. Immediately the three diamonds were Father, Jesus, and the Holy Spirit, and the engravings were the Vine and the branches. From that day until this moment, I have worn this ring on my right-hand ring finger.

I do not believe that God singled me out or gave me something that He wouldn't do for someone else. Since 1999 I have met other persons who have seen Jesus. Also, I am daily with friends and colleagues who openly share with one another what the Lord Jesus says to them and how they respond to Him. I feel like the blind beggar, Bartimaeus (Mark 10:46) who kept calling out "Jesus, Son of David, have mercy on me!" over and over until Jesus stopped walking, stood still, and commanded that he be brought into His Presence, and He healed him. I further believe that in my desperate, single-minded calling out that night, I reached a kind of critical mass and fulfilled what is stated in Jeremiah 29:13, "And you will seek Me and find Me, when you search for Me with all your heart."

Reflecting on the End of an Era

Through prayer and conversations with friends, I have come to internalize two major realities of this event: death and ownership.

Death. Something in me needed to die, though the literal sense of death that grabbed me that night was a distortion. From my early childhood I had internalized a sense of entitlement. I was chosen, special, part of the elite corps of priests-in-training in the seminary. Then, in the doctrine of humanism, I had built on this early ego-inflation by believing that *my human self was a master*. In New Age spirituality and in transpersonal psychology, I had accepted a further extension of egocentricity by adorning this *self* with divinity.

On the negative side of the ledger, I believe there was a reactionary ego-state, which I have called a *survivor-self*, formed as a reaction to having my life programmed for me from birth. When I lost the priest identity, this survivor-self became even more entrenched. Its basic belief was: *You have to take care of yourself because no one else will. You're on your own.*

I believe that the ego-inflation plus the survivor-self produced in me a consolidated sense of self-ownership. Much of this self-structure had been broken open, shattered, and dismantled from 1984 to 1999. However, back in Brightmoor Tabernacle, on that Sunday in 1984, I had the clear sense that choosing the Person who said "I am Life" was an all-or-nothing choice, not an amalgam of His Life and myself-as-life.

1998 and 1999 were difficult years as this residue of my entrenched self was stripped away. Things were happening beyond my control and I needed others to cope. I felt like a patient in an intensive-care ward. The hospital was my church, the Fellowship of Christ; the doctors and nurses were church members and close friends.

I came to realize God's healing love through the care of many in my spiritual family, partly through their encouragement and comfort, and partly through strong "medicine." One day I received a note from my pastor's wife, Sheila, in which she quoted Jesus in John 12:24 NASB: "Truly, truly, I say to you, unless a grain of wheat falls into the earth and dies, it remains alone; but if it dies, it bears much fruit." She coupled this dose of truth with words of love, encouragement, and assurance of continued prayer for my wellbeing. The medicine was God's truth about puffed up pride of self—let it go, let it be reckoned as dead. This truth was being dispensed daily through one of the best medicines for the soul known to mankind: learning humility by being humbled.

On February 19, 1999 I believe that a death occurred. My hidden "grain" was squeezed out into the open and fell down in desperation... falling on the ground at His feet...humbly calling out to the real King. In receiving His invitation to abide in Him, as a pre-taste of the wedding feast of the Book of Revelation, the *solo* in me died.

Previously, as depicted in my Galatians 4:7 story, I had come to experientially know my identity as a son in the Kingdom. Now I knew a deeper, truer reality—that I was a son in the Son. My son-identity did not exist in isolation or apart from Jesus, and I knew that there was no place for a self-pedestal in my intimate relationship with Him.

From that time forward, in a more experiential way, my sense of identity became Jesus-*in*-me, more than Jesus *and* me. From now on I would have more of an inner, felt-sense that the "I am Life," initially experienced as Father God, included Jesus ("I am the Way, the Truth, and the Life"). In the years to come I would deepen that inner experience of "I am Life" to include the Holy Spirit as well.

Ownership. The underlying beliefs of my old self were: *I am my own person; I do things my way; I have to take care of myself; I am an individual unto myself; I am the boss; I own myself.* Many of those beliefs had been challenged and dismantled prior to 1999. But after 1999 there was a new awareness to grow into. I had known and had accepted that redemption meant God had "bought me back," and that I belonged to Him. But now I was more experientially aware of the radical nature of redemption.

Part of my medicinal dose of humility during the last two years of the century was the realization that I was a small creature in the hands of a very large and powerful God. Yet I came to realize by experience that this Master did not want to possess me like a master possesses a slave. He wanted me to be a member of His family in a very intimate way. This involved the grafting of me into Him...like a branch grafted into a vine. He was not saying "Behave and do what you're told!" He was lovingly saying "Be Mine."

I began to know "It is no longer I who lives but Christ lives in me" (Gal. 2:20) as an exchange of ownership. I would no longer be self-possessed. By the year 2000 I had fully agreed to that exchange. I handed over the deed of my life and began to learn at a deeper level what that meant.

Let me be quick to say that I still struggle with reckoning that my old self is dead. *Self* regularly jumps in and acts independently and selfishly, but it is no longer in position to be dominant for long. Let me also be quick to say that this lessening of self-dominance does not remove a sense of personal responsibility for the damage I caused others, as mentioned in Chapter 3.

My self-identity has been altered in the following ways: I don't belong to myself, I belong to God. I was created by Him, and He has purposes for me in this world and beyond. I am committed to learn whatever it takes to stay aligned and in agreement with Him so that these purposes will be realized. He is my Master and I am His servant/apprentice.

I am completely content and at peace with these terms of our relationship. I thank God daily for His mercy and love in making such a plan possible.

Chapter 6

Called Up to the Majors

On January 1, 2000 I moved from my apartment into a duplex managed by a family in my church. My sons Adrian and John lived in Chapel Hill, and my son Adam lived in California. They visited on a regular basis, and I also made trips to California. I was learning how to father but I was a single dad and had very little mentoring in how to be a father. My father had been a relationally distant man, and he was more of a guardian than a parent—just taking care of me until I was turned over to the priests in the seminary at age 14. These celibate men who had no children of their own were my "fathers" for many years (Sometimes now it seems like the seminary was a kind of semi-orphanage.). In 2000 I was at a new stage in my life and had much to learn about fathering and about other purposes God had in store for me.

Throughout all of the difficulties of 1999, I would occasionally hear a quiet voice from within, calming me with loving assurance that He would take care of me. It was a voice of truth. God did provide for me in many ways and I came to know experientially aspects and names of God that previously had been more cognitive and conceptual. I now *experienced* Him as my Provider, my Shelter from the storm, my Hiding Place, my Deliverer, my Healer, my Strength, my Provider, my Father, my Savior, my Friend, my Comforter. So many biblical descriptors of God were now proven to be true. My faith grew, my trust deepened, and a desire increased to serve out the purposes God had for me.

Like the sky clearing as clouds drift away after a storm, I felt more free and clear than ever before. The allegation against me in my therapy practice was found to be without merit and was dismissed. The Fellowship of Christ asked me to join their staff, commissioning me as a minister of Pastoral Care. I was put in charge of counseling and the various ministries of Care in the church. I was given a new office and joined the team of pastors who served the congregation.

Because of my own healing and what I had witnessed in Nancy, Mary, and others, I was poised to move beyond traditional counseling into effective healing as led by the Holy Spirit. A group of us with a similar interest formed the nucleus of what we called "inner healing ministry." We had done some reading, experimented with some unstructured inner healing, and prayed together for direction. We became aware of Ed Smith and his Theophostic Prayer Ministry (TPM). Theophostic (God's light illumining) was a strange word but Dr. Smith's core ideas caught our attention. We ordered his teaching materials and began our own training group.

Several aspects of TPM struck me as significant. First of all, Ed Smith had been a Christian counselor and had grown weary of treating symptoms, doing what he called "tolerable recovery." After a late-night prayer of desperation, God clearly showed him that He desired *direct* involvement in the healing process. I too had experienced that desire of God to be the Healer, not a silent Observer who opens and closes counseling sessions. I was now convinced that healing was God's business, not ours. Ed Smith understood that we are to be assistants and facilitators, not in-charge counselors.

Secondly, God had shown Ed the truth about the power of lies, especially embedded, buried lies. And He had shown Ed that it is the Holy Spirit who searches the depths of our hearts, bringing out into the open what needs to be exposed (1 Cor. 2:10-11). Then, in an exchange-process, the lie or false belief is released, replaced by truth that flows from the mind of Christ by the power of the Holy Spirit. To me these were not fancy, idealistic thoughts; the basic process of TPM resonated with my soul. I had experienced exactly this exchange of truth for lies as had some of the members of our inner healing team at the Fellowship of Christ. We began to learn the principles of TPM and to do ministry with one another.

Thirdly, in describing what makes facilitators effective, TPM had a key insight that we took to heart: Facilitators need to undergo healing themselves to prevent blocking the healing process of their ministry recipients. As we ministered to one another, and began to minister to others in the church, we found this to be true. For example: a facilitator has a father who repeatedly called him "stupid" when he was a child and has internalized a belief that *I don't have what it takes to succeed.* In all likelihood his unresolved pain from that experience will be triggered and he will feel uncomfortable when doing ministry with someone who shares similar childhood pain—perhaps without him even realizing the source of his discomfort.

What Ed Smith noticed, as did we, is that the ministry facilitator, when personally triggered, is likely to redirect the session from the feelings and beliefs of the recipient back into a more comfortable (for the facilitator) cognitive mode—as a means of self-protection. In effect, the healing that the Holy Spirit might have intended is derailed by discomfort in the facilitator. Our motto became: Stay committed to continue receiving your own healing so you can effectively minister to others.

More Stories of Real Healing

Becoming visible. In a ministry session I was facilitating, the recipient felt *misunderstood and invisible,* and he was connecting with those feelings. I felt my own discomfort and clumsily jerked the session from the emotional to the intellectual realm, effectively derailing the process. Adhering to our ministry's adopted motto, I sought healing from two team members.

We gathered together in a room and began by prayer and then by anchoring me in the feelings associated with "misunderstood" and "invisible." In praying for the Holy Spirit to reveal the origin of these feelings, an old photo of me in the front of Holy Rosary Church in Detroit Lakes, Minnesota came to mind. I was about seven years old and had just completed my First Communion. I was standing dressed in a white shirt, white pants, and a tie. My godmother was crouched beside me, holding my arm, and my priest-uncle crouched at my other side holding my other arm. In the photo I have a wan smile on my face. I was going along with the whole program but they were holding onto a boy they saw as their "little priest." I felt invisible and trapped inside. The phrase "That's not me" came as I gazed at this photo-image in my mind. Rising from this memory were feelings of anxiety and anger. I was in agreement with the ministry facilitators as they prayed for the Holy Spirit to show me what was going on.

Thoughts emerged from the feelings in the memories: "I had no choice" and "How could you do that to somebody?!" My submerged charge of anger came out against my parents, and my godparents. The whole priest-thing had been put on me as my *identity* but there was a human boy named Billy who was invisible and had to stay hidden under the priest-to-be identity.

Now we prayed for God to show me what He wanted me to know from His perspective. I opened my heart and waited. In my mind, a light came into my First Communion picture. Words came: "You are My son and I see you." Tears of relief flowed. I no longer felt invisible there. *The Lord was there all the time.* I had a surrounding sense of that truth within me. Amazed, I accepted and released the anger, and the feelings of being invisible, trapped, coerced. I forgave my family and released everything to the Lord.

There was more healing to do about my underlying sense of being invisible, but this session was enough to enable me to continue with my recipient and not derail the process.

From rejection to liberation. A couple of years later, in another inner healing session, the Holy Spirit brought out into the open a buried interpretation I had formed as to why I had to leave the seminary. The interpretation was tied into my belief about *not measuring up*.

The time was ripe for surgically removing this cancerous growth in my soul. I had just returned from a pastors' retreat in which a discussion about my role in the church had gone awry, mostly because I had been triggered and swamped with feelings and thoughts about *being mis-understood*. These thoughts opened up into feeling *isolated, alienated, and being an outcast*. Something big was about to appear out of the mist. I could tell because I felt so anxious and uncomfortable...yet I wanted to know the truth.

My ministry facilitator and I began by having me review and re-experience my emotions and thoughts as they emerged in the discussion with the pastors. Feelings of anger, rejection, and anxiety stood out. Coming forward out of these feelings were thoughts of *not measuring up, not belonging,* and *being on the outside.* The feelings and thoughts were much stronger than what might have been generated by the discussion at the retreat, and my facilitator and I prayed to know their origin.

After a few moments a memory emerged of a time in my 20s when I was visiting my parents in Minnesota. One night I had mustered the courage to walk into my father's bedroom. The lights were dimmed and he was lying in bed winding down before going to sleep. I had never heard an "I love you" (or anything close to that) from him and, for whatever reason, it was stirred up inside me to ask him what he thought of me. There had been an uncomfortable void in my heart for years and I hoped he might fill it in a satisfying way.

I can't even remember his reply when I asked him what he thought of me because it was so indirect and deflective. I walked out of his bedroom deflated, more empty than before I entered, wishing I had not asked him. The pain from that memory flooded into my awareness in the ministry session and I prayed for further guidance: What did the Lord want me to know by bringing up this memory?

Immediately in my mind I was back in the seminary, strongly experiencing the belief that *I didn't measure up...I didn't have the right stuff...I didn't make the grade.* I had been a diligent student, salutatorian and valedictorian of my high school and college classes, respectively, so I was surprised by this last belief about not making the grade.

Then something like a trap door in my mind opened and the beliefs I had buried as to why I left the seminary swept forward into full consciousness. The beliefs: *God had decided I didn't have what it took to be in His elite corps of priests. I had been cut from the team. I wasn't good enough. I didn't come up to the grade-level of worthiness to be in the select few. He had taken away my vocation to be a priest. God had rejected me.* Now all the buried hurt and pain roared out onto the center stage of my mind and heart. Even though the pain had been stored in my heart for years, when it emerged it had a burning, searing energy as though it were a fresh wound. Sobbing, I held it all up to the Lord and asked for His truth, for what He wanted me to know about those beliefs.

Into my mind came the words MINOR and MAJOR. The first eight years of seminary (high school and college) were called "minor seminary," and the last four years of theology training were called "major seminary." I saw that for many years I had believed that I wasn't good enough for the major seminary, that I was only good enough for the *minor league* of the minor seminary. I believed that I had been cut from the "A" team.

With this revelation, the Holy Spirit then beckoned me to release all of these old beliefs to Him as He now poured in thoughts of His perspective: I had not been found unworthy. I had not been cut because I did not have the right stuff. God hadn't rejected me; He had released and liberated me so I could move toward what He had in store for me in His mentoring of me. He has been grooming and preparing me for such a time as this, right here in North Carolina. The major league was not the major seminary. I am in *His* major league now because I am in what He has called me to. I measure up because I am in Him and He is equipping me for my calling. I may receive and accept that I have been called up to the majors."

With great relief and tears of joy I allowed the Lord to make the exchange of His truth for the long-held lies, and a comforting peace settled into every part of me that had been so distraught.

My calling was reinforced after that inner healing. I understood "His major league" not to mean major in the sense of more important or superior; it was major because it was what *He* wanted me to be doing.

Chapter 7

Learning to Assist The Master

A Second Ring to go with the First

2000 to 2003 was a time of deepening in my relationship with the Lord. He was more Master of my life than ever before. There was also a growing intimacy through my daily communion times with Him and through the exchanges that occurred in my healing prayer times. More and more I was at peace, learning for the first time the joy and satisfaction of "delighting myself in the Lord" and seeking His Kingdom above all else. There had been no romantic interest in this new century and I did not know if I would ever marry again. I knew I could live out my days without a mate, and it would be ok. I desired to have a life-long companion but if that desire was to be fulfilled I wanted God involved this time.

In 2002 three women from my church went to Argentina on a mission trip. They had traveled together with a group of women from a sister church in Charlotte, North Carolina. While in Argentina, each of the women from my church, independent of one another, thought of me while talking to one of the women from the Charlotte church, and mentioned me by name to her. When the three women returned to Cary each one called me, telling me about their encounter with a member of the Charlotte team by name of Susan.

One of the Cary women planned a time for us to meet, and we agreed to this arrangement. In January, 2003 we met in a church home-group in Raleigh. Susan was in a solid relationship with the Lord and she had received inner healing in her Charlotte church, experiencing much freedom from the sessions. After the evening in January we met for breakfast and had a long conversation. Subsequent to this talk, we both felt led by the Lord to get to know one another. As we took our cues from Him rather than from our selves or from "chemistry," the relationship progressed gradually and steadily. Within three months we came to believe that the Lord was calling us to marry. Our friend Pat, who had introduced us to one another, became one of our wedding planners. We tell everyone that we had an "arranged marriage," and truly it seems so!

On November 15, 2003 we married in the sanctuary of the Fellowship of Christ. In our exchange of vows we promised to help one another stay faithful to the *first Love* of our lives, the Lord Jesus. Then we exchanged our vows to one another in what we called our *second love*. Susan's children, Laurie and Matt, were present along with my sons Adam, Adrian, and John. We became a family of seven.

Susan and I had the usual awkward adjustments in the early years of our marriage, but we are now ten years married and have developed a strong bond of love and trust. The Lord is our "third strand in a cord that cannot be broken," and each of us now wears two rings, one on each hand. The ring on Susan's right hand has the same significance as the ring on my right hand (described in Chapter Five).

Our marriage has been a wonderful surprise for both of us. We have a strong spiritual connection in the Lord, and together we have pursued further healing and training through the inner healing ministry of the Fellowship of Christ. We are thankful for God's goodness, His mercy, and His love. We are happy together and hope to live out His purposes for our lives.

Healing Troubled Hearts: More training

In 2006 our inner healing team at Fellowship of Christ drove to Virginia to attend a three-day training in Theophostic Prayer Ministry, given by Ed Smith, the founder of the ministry. He had seemed to disappear from the scene for the previous few years and we wanted to see what he now had to say. I could see a changed man (from the one I had seen in his previous DVDs) standing before us with humble candor, sharing that he had gone through extensive inner healing himself. He had repressed some painful events in his life for a long time, and he finally let the Lord deal with those areas of his soul.

From his experiences of how God had healed him he had written a new book and training materials. During those three days, as I watched person after person volunteer to receive a ministry session with Dr. Smith, I sensed how intense God's desire is to engage us in meaningful dialogue so that He can change out lies and replace them with His healing truth. In my heart, God's title of *Jehovah Rapha* (the God who heals) was becoming more real and true.

In 2008 I attended a three-day conference in Moravian Falls, North Carolina. It was called *Healing for the Brokenhearted*. The leader of the training was a man named Andy Miller who would become an important mentor for me in ensuing years. He was a licensed clinical social worker with a practice focused on helping severely traumatized people.

In his work with emotional trauma, he had observed that there is a protective, guardian-like part of one's personality that forms within the soul to keep reservoirs of trauma-pain from continually flooding consciousness. This is called *dissociation*. With this pain held at bay, a traumatized person is then able to function in daily life.

Although Andy worked mostly with severely traumatized persons, such as victims of sexual or physical abuse, he observed that many people go through events in life that don't get fully resolved or processed at the time of emotionally disturbing incidents. They then protect themselves by pushing the pain away—a milder form of dissociation—in order to function in daily tasks. I found this information intriguing, especially as I watched Andy facilitate actual ministry sessions.

During a break, while I was on a walk pondering the content of the seminar about this "protector," I actually felt a strongly protective part of myself. It was an experiential discovery that dissolved the skepticism I had been harboring. I began to observe this part of my soul.

Also present at the seminar was Ed Khouri who had been tracking new developments in brain science that confirmed much of what Andy was teaching. Ed mentioned publications and research coming out of Shepherd's House, a Christian ministry and training organization that was interested in both brain science and inner healing ministry. One of the researchers and authors mentioned was Dr. James Wilder who called himself a "neurotheologian."

Towards the end of the seminar, the whole group discussed the evident development of a new and growing network in the field of Christian inner healing. It was exciting to feel part of a larger plan that was unfolding.

Naming and Reclaiming

Around this time, our team wrestled with giving a proper name to our ministry. Because there was a wide spectrum of meanings for the term *inner healing*, we seriously considered getting rid of the term altogether. Many New Age/New Spirituality counselors and therapists had adopted the term, imbuing it with multiple meanings. *Inner* might refer to Carl Jung's collective unconscious, reincarnation memories, or a spiritual realm in which angelic beings were "inner guides."

In the 1960s through the 1980s the term was taken up by several ministers of healing who "Christianized" it. These included Ruth Carter Stapleton, John and Paula Sandford, Francis MacNutt, David Seamands, and others. The meanings for *inner healing* were greatly narrowed by the biblical understanding imparted to *soul* and *spirit*, but controversy raged about whether or not Christ-centered inner healing was biblically-based ministry and therapy or unscriptural "psychoheresy." The controversy continues today.

While deliberating about a name, our ministry-team researched the word *inner* to see if it was found in the Bible. Our findings were surprising.

In the Old Testament, The Hebrew words for "inward parts" can refer to the bowels or breast, or sometimes the viscera (heart, liver, kidneys). Ancient wisdom linked these bodily locations to the seat of the mind, emotions, affections, or the soul. Sometimes the spiritual dimension is meant, as in "wisdom in the inward parts" (Job 38:36), or "My law in their inward parts" (Jeremiah 31:36).

In the New Testament, the terms "inward man," "the internal man," or "the inner man" (Romans 7:22; 2 Cor. 4:16; Ephesians 3:16) refer to mind, soul, and spirit—as distinguished from the outward man, the visible body (*International Standard Bible Encyclopedia*, 1988).

Most relevant, however, and a finding that riveted our attention, was learning that the stand-alone Hebrew word for "inner" most often referred to the temple. In Solomon's Temple, there were three courts: the outer court, the inner court, and the innermost (inner of inner) court. The latter was also referred to as the "Inner Sanctuary" or "the Most Holy Place"—the place where God dwelled (See 1 Kings 6:16).

In the New Testament the meaning of temple goes even deeper. 1 Cor. 3:16 says, "Don't you know that you yourselves are God's temple, and that God's Spirit lives in you...? For God's temple is sacred, and you are that temple." For us, the concept of a believer's body, soul, and spirit corresponded, respectively, to the outer court, inner court, and inner sanctuary of the temple.

Putting all of this together and praying over the matter, we realized that *inner* was a deeply meaningful, biblical word, and we wanted to reclaim it, not discard it. The healing that we believed we were called to was exactly this inner realm of soul and spirit in humans, whom we believed were created to be temples of God. Here in soul and spirit, humans were heartbroken, oppressed, and bound up in shame and fear. We knew and had experienced that God intended healing and restoration in this inner realm of human nature.

In the end we chose *Isaiah 61 Ministry* as our name because of the many phrases in Chapter 61 of the Book of Isaiah that delineate the process of exchange so clearly. The Chapter begins with "The Spirit of the Lord God is upon Me..." and then indicates that this Spirit gives beauty for ashes, joy in place of mourning, honor to replace shame...all coming out of this same Spirit of God as He "heals the brokenhearted... proclaims liberty to the imprisoned...and gives relief to those weighed down by heavy burdens." These *exchanges* by the Holy Spirit were precisely what we felt called to facilitate in our sessions with the brokenhearted, depressed, and anxious persons who were coming to us for healing and peace.

Further, these verses in Isaiah 61, real though we believed them to be, were actually a foreshadowing of Jesus, the fulfillment and full truth of all these exchanges.

For many years the verses of the Bible that have literally given me shivers are in Luke 4:16-21. Jesus had just returned from 40 days of fasting and prayer in the desert. He walked into the synagogue of

Nazareth on the Sabbath day and stood up to read. As a noted Rabbi, that would not have been an uncommon occurrence. He was handed the scroll of the Book of Isaiah. He immediately went to Chapter 61 and began to read: "The Spirit of the Lord is upon Me..." and continued reading the passages about healing the brokenhearted, freeing prisoners and the oppressed, etc. Then (this is the part that always gets to me) He handed the scroll back to the attendant, and sat down. A pause followed...everyone was looking at Him. Then Jesus said to them, "Today this Scripture is fulfilled in your hearing." In other words He was saying that the "Me" of "The Spirit of the Lord is upon Me" is Himself. Can you imagine sitting in that hushed synagogue when this event occurred and Jesus said that?

With this Christ-realized understanding of the Isaiah verses, *Isaiah 61 Prayer Ministry* became a perfect name to designate the co-laboring to which God had called us. And because of the fruit of our research, we were at peace with referring to Isaiah 61 Ministry as inner healing. To this day we retain Isaiah 61 as the proper name of our ministry, but interchangeably use the terms inner healing, healing prayer, or listening prayer.

From this point on, whenever you see the term *inner healing,* please understand that the explanation above is the context for the meaning I intend. For me, using the term *inner healing* is a way of taking back and reclaiming land that was God-given in the first place.

More Healing, Training...and Brain Science

In 2010 I received several inner healing sessions from Andy Miller at Tallahassee Healing Prayer Ministries in Florida. During the first session it was clear that my *protector* was guarded about allowing Andy or the Lord access to a deep reservoir of pain from my early childhood. This gatekeeper-part of my soul was wary of anyone who might cause more pain. "Billy" had already suffered enough in having to be invisible for an entire childhood while the priest-to-be identity had almost always been on center stage for everyone to see and acknowledge.

Andy deftly facilitated a dialogue whereby that protective part of me heard words of love and tenderness from the Lord. Trust was established, something guarded in me eased up and opened a gate, and long-held tears flowed out in a gush of release. Some healing had already taken place (described in Chapter 6) but a deeper layer was now released, and the Master spoke into that hidden part: "You are in Me, you are visible to Me and in Me."

In my three days with Andy Miller I was introduced to a new ministry through Andy adapting into his inner healing protocol what was called the *Immanuel approach. Immanuel* (God with us) was developed by a Christian psychiatrist, Dr. Karl Lehman, and his wife Charlotte. Dr. Lehman had become frustrated in his efforts toward helping severely traumatized patients receive healing because they would often feel so uncomfortable that they would emotionally disconnect from a traumatic memory.

In an answer to prayer for guidance, he had a sense to refocus a current patient away from the problem and onto just being in the presence of Jesus. Dr. Lehman followed this directive and the patient was then able to stay emotionally connected in the memory and receive healing. Dr. Lehman gives the analogy of a small child told to go down into a dark basement. She is afraid of the dark and will not go down. However, if her father takes her hand and goes down the basement stairs with her, she will comply.

Dr. Lehman was already involved with Ed Khouri, Dr. Jim Wilder, and others in examining brain science discoveries. They were coming to understand that the severity of trauma impedes the ability to stay emotionally connected inside of its memory. Dr. Lehman discovered that the presence of the Lord *gives the capacity* one needs to stay emotionally connected, and thereby be able to release the disturbing emotions and receive healing within the memory.

I had read some of Dr. Lehman's website articles, but now I experienced his approach in my sessions with Andy. I realized how much the Lord wants to heal in a context of personally relating to recipients. In one post-session discussion, Andy pointed out an enormous deficiency of attachment and bonding in my childhood. The Lord had addressed this trauma by the loving, welcoming warmth of

His Presence. Andy's observation rang true within me; I felt more whole-hearted and less relationally detached than when I first arrived in Tallahassee.

One further point about brain science. Previously I have spoken of dealing with lies and wrong interpretations beneath the top layer of the mind. New light has been shed on the functions of the brain through magnetic resonance imaging (MRI). Turns out it is not top or lower layers as much as it is left or right hemispheres. The left side of the brain is where reasoning, logic, and analysis take place. We store words and explanations here; it is like a *library*. The right brain is non-verbal, imaginative, visual, and knows things by experiencing them.

When we are emotionally triggered, in order to deal with the current situation the right brain turns off the left brain and taps consciousness into what a person has learned from past experiences. Cognitive therapies aimed at changing behavior by teaching strategies and conflict-resolution skills are of limited effectiveness because these are all information-concepts stored in the library part (left hemisphere) of the brain—which is shut off during an emotional upheaval. Interpretations, beliefs, and emotions are all woven into the experiences processed in the right brain—the area that must be accessed in order to facilitate effective change.

I returned to the Isaiah 61 leadership team in North Carolina to give a presentation of the healing and training I had received. From my healing experience and from the brain-science information described above, I felt confident in confirming that our ministry in North Carolina was heading in a good direction.

Chapter 8

In the Hands of The Potter

From what I was learning about resolving issues and exchanging beliefs in the experiential right-brain, it seemed more and more futile to be shuffling around thoughts in the cognition-storehouse of the left brain or tinkering with behavior that was really coming from internal, negative beliefs.[2]

By 2008, for those patients who were ready and could receive it, I functioned as a surgical assistant to the Master Surgeon who removed cancerous soul-growths of lies, wrongful interpretations of events, and hidden sins. He then filled those places in the soul with His love, truth, assurance, forgiveness and peace.

My M.A. in theology now meant *Master's Assistant*. I facilitated the encounters between recipients and the Lord and listened to the Holy Spirit's direction. I also developed the habit of silently praying for guidance throughout the entire healing session—a move away from giving advice, knowledge, and strategies from my mind. More and more I wanted to assist in creating an atmosphere within the room in which persons could hear, sense, and know what truth the Lord specifically desired to impart in any given moment.[3]

Toward the end of 2008, during times of prayer, the Holy Spirit repeatedly impressed upon me that I was to return to private practice in a clinical setting. For 15 years I had been going through my own healing and training in faith-based ministry. I processed this change with the

---

[2] It should be noted that counseling and psychotherapy are not bereft of methods to access experiential knowledge. For example, Eye Movement Desensitization and Reprocessing (EMDR) and some new techniques for treating trauma in war-injured military personnel go directly into the actual traumatic memories. These approaches are proving to be helpful.

[3] I believe there is validity to traditional Christian counseling, and I sometimes shift into the role of counselor—to be discussed in Ch. 20.

pastoral staff and the elders of the Fellowship of Christ. One evening, in a warm and encouraging assembly of colleagues and friends, I was prayerfully sent out with their blessing, as they asked God to continue to build His Kingdom through the work He was giving me to do.

From 2009 until today in 2014, I have been a member of Ridgeview Counseling Associates, in Cary, North Carolina. One of the co-owners of the practice has become an iron-sharpening-iron brother and friend. I also enjoy the collegial camaraderie of the other associates in the practice. I resigned my position at the Fellowship of Christ but remain as a member of and consultant to Isaiah 61 Ministry, and sometimes facilitate ministry sessions for recipients at the church.

Who am I?

I call my private practice Deep Healing Psychotherapy. In my disclosure statement and in my initial talks with prospective patients, I freely disclose what I do. I discuss with patients the role of prayer and accessing God's perspective through their faith. I also describe to them the basic process of exchanging truth for lies. The process of inner healing is easily adapted to a clinical setting. The basic therapeutic process is the exchange of healthy, positive beliefs in place of negative, defeating beliefs—a replacement that occurs within memories of traumatic experiences.

Perhaps my family of origin was given a glimpse of God's purposes and made the only interpretation that made sense to them within their culture of Roman Catholicism. I don't know, but I have accepted it all— from conception on—as the unfolding of God's plan. I have accepted the pieces as fit by Him into His larger plan. He is The Potter, I am the clay, and as I let the clay rest in His hands, He will shape it into a vessel of His design and purpose.

The Potter shapes the pieces to fit together in the vessel He is making, but extraneous material is sometimes scraped off and tossed out. Much of what I learned in my trainings as a social worker, psychologist, and even Christian counselor has been discarded. But I learned helpful skills that have enabled me to navigate in the vast realm of the soul: how to listen; how to respect and value each person's life-story; how to understand the interrelatedness of thinking, feeling, and willing; how to recognize signs of trauma, addiction, depression, and other soul maladies. Also, familiarity with *The Diagnostic and Statistical Manual of Mental Disorders* has sometimes been useful in knowing how to proceed with certain problems.

I am not enamored with the value of having professional training, licenses, certifications, or brain lobes stuffed with tomes of information from established schools of higher learning. And I believe the Holy Spirit can use lay and clergy alike in ministry. If He calls someone for service, He will provide what they need, which *may* mean training and other types of equipping. But I believe the major equipping is in the *call*, i.e., the Holy Spirit's anointing and commissioning of a person for service. Our Isaiah 61 ministry team is made up of a nurse, a pastor, an entrepreneur, a life-coach, a licensed Christian counselor, an ordained deacon, and a homemaker.

God continues to mold and shape whatever I give Him. I have been a small-town boy from Minnesota, a Catholic seminarian, a university theology instructor, a humanistic social worker, a transpersonal psychologist, a Christian counselor, a pastor of counseling and inner healing ministry...and now a hybrid psychotherapist/minister with an office in a secular setting for therapy and an office in a church setting for inner healing ministry. I surrender all of this to the Lord, for Him to use as He will in accomplishing His purposes.

Finally, and most essentially, I believe I have been called to the ministry of Reconciliation, as given in 2 Cor. 5:19: "God was in Christ reconciling the world to Himself." I will take up this complete text in Chapter 10—it is the core of everything I have to say. For now I mention it in passing. This Reconciliation Ministry is, I believe, the broader context and the vocation of all who would call themselves believers. In one co-labor or another, following Jesus means to accept God's invitation to join Him in reconciling the world to Himself.

Knowing Who I am is Knowing *Whose* I am

I bring PART I to a close by recounting an inner healing I received about two years ago. If you recall (Chapter 6, *Called Up to the Majors*), as a young adult I had gone into my father's bedroom while on a vacation visit seeking to be affirmed by him. I came away empty and unblessed. I received some healing in that memory when the Lord showed me that *in Him* I had the right stuff to be successful in life as a man. And previously in the 1990s, I had received those marvelous, life-giving words: "You are no longer a slave, you are My son." But something was missing, and I became aware of this through a member of our inner healing team.

Bill V., a Christian therapist on our inner healing team, had done some training in an inner healing ministry called SOZO (a Greek word for *saved, healed, restored*). One of the tools in SOZO is named the *Father Ladder*. It initially helps a person discern if he or she perceives *relational distance* with Father, Jesus, or the Holy Spirit. As Bill talked about this method during a presentation of what he had learned from his training, I realized that I felt distance between myself and my heavenly Father, even though I had experiential assurance of being His son. I prayed on the matter and then asked Bill and Pastor Greg to administer a healing time for me.

On the appointed day we met in a room in which many healing prayer sessions had occurred. We began by acknowledging the presence of the Lord in our midst. I closed my eyes to bring my awareness to an inward focus on Immanuel, God with us. Along with sensing the presence of God, a visual of a large heart appeared front and center in my mind. The heart was radiating love and warmth, and I knew Father, Jesus, and the Holy Spirit were symbolized in this heart-image. I felt close to Jesus and the Holy Spirit, but the Father-aspect of the heart was somewhat removed—almost like a separate segment.

When I indicated the distance I felt between Father and myself, Bill prayed and asked the Holy Spirit to reveal why the distance was there. Immediately the memory of going into my father's bedroom came forward in my mind. I was surprised because of the healing I had previously received in that memory. Bill asked for the Holy Spirit to expose any lie in that memory. Slowly I realized that the pain I had felt from my father's tepid words about what he thought of me caused a rift of mistrust to form inside.

I had mustered up the courage to reach out to my dad, and emptiness and pain were the result. In a flash I saw that I had projected this trust-rift onto my heavenly Father: *I didn't fully trust that He would be there for me if I reached out to Him.* For years I had been keeping some distance from Him, believing that He might be like my father...and I might come away hurt and empty from any encounter with Him.

Bill asked if I was willing to forgive my dad for causing that pain, to renounce the belief I had projected onto my heavenly Father, and to ask forgiveness for having falsely accused Him. I had known the truth of God's goodness for several years and wanted the "cancerous growth" of this lie to be removed. I was willing, and I did all three actions out loud.

We then prayed for the Holy Spirit to fill that place in my soul with His truth. After a short while the image of the radiating heart returned to mind, only now Father, Jesus, and the Holy Spirit were firmly together. The distance and the rift were gone. The oneness and unity of the heart became a symbol charged with energy as I experienced an inner rush of the three separate "segments" flowing into a unified whole.

The best description I can think of is that it was like a spiritual chiropractic adjustment whereby something that had been misaligned in my soul was now in place. The "adjustment" had a solid ring of truth to it and I felt reconciled to my earthly father and to my Heavenly Father. The distance was gone and has not returned.

I felt ready to receive a blessing from my Father and in that moment knew why I had been impressed to invite Pastor Greg into the healing session. He had been on the inner healing team in our early days when we were facilitating and receiving ministry from one another. Greg had received powerful healing regarding his manhood and was now a *father* to many young men who had father-wounds. His anointing was, and is, to bring the Good News of the love of the Father to hearts which need precisely that aspect of the Godhead.

Greg stood over me as I was seated, and he put one hand on my heart and the other hand on my shoulder. He began to pray down the love of the Father to pour into my soul and for me to receive His affirmation, His truth, and everything He had for me. By now I was like a sponge, ready to soak it all up. It was like a deep, deep hole inside being filled with love, warmth, and life. Years of sadness released through copious tears; and the same flow of tears expressed relief as I welcomed refreshing, living Water into my soul. My arms were outstretched, as though standing beneath a waterfall, and I received the father-blessing I had been longing for, my whole life-long.

I received and embraced Father's words that came through Greg: *He would always be there for me; I was His beloved son; He would never let go of me even if I let go of my hold on Him; I was firmly in His hands.*

And then, suddenly, Aslan, the lion from C.S. Lewis' Narnia stories, was standing there in my imagination. In *The Chronicles of Narnia*, Aslan always represents the Lord Jesus, but as the Lion stood there in my mind's eye, I saw that Aslan was also the Father. I had not thought of that before in regard to Aslan, though I knew Jesus had told Philip (and all of us): "He who has seen me has seen the Father..." (John 14:9). This image of the Father within Aslan was confirmation that my Father-rift was gone, the distance was gone, and the lie was gone.

I saw that, quite simply, Jesus is the loving heart of the Father and that the Father, like Aslan, is *wild*...but He is *good*. I confessed aloud that indeed our Father is truly Lovingkindness, the name He gave to Himself in the Word over and over, in the years before Jesus brought this Lovingkindness deeply into all of creation.

Part II

From Brokenness to Wholeness: An Initial Look at Restoration

Chapter 9

Repair or Replace: Addressing a Fundamental Question

I have encountered many variations of soul-maladies in my work over the years, but for the most part they reflect disturbances in relationships. Having healthy bonding and secure attachments in one's early years doesn't guarantee a problem-free life, but a disruption or absence of these factors can crack and crumble the foundations of human life like nothing else. Persons broken by abandonment and abuse learn to cope, to manage, to adjust—to develop a *survivor-self*. But such fundamental damage is difficult to heal.

My patient, Nancy (Chapter 4), did not know her father in her childhood, and her attachment bonds with her disturbed and addicted mother were very thin. She had been abandoned by her mother at four years of age, and her aunt and uncle provided minimal bonding for her. Nancy's descriptions of her childhood showed all of the symptoms of separation anxiety.

In my case, a lack of attachment to my parents and my threadbare sense of belonging with my family and childhood peers resulted in generalized anxiety. Insecurity and anxiety were almost constant companions throughout my life, until I met the Lord and was taken into a secure relationship with Him.

I have developed a conviction that *humans were made for relationship*. Bonding, belonging, attachment, friendship, and intimacy are the most fundamental aspects of our very being. Yet, as I look at how human life unfolds for many people, I see that their dreams and desires of successful, harmonious relationships become shattered sooner or later, and sometimes right from the start. When heart-wholeness is broken, it can be patched up and repaired, but restoration to wholeness is rare.

Healing *began* for me when I finally acknowledged that I was primarily made for relationship with God. Healing *grew* by allowing Him to restore me to right relationship with Him, and with others.

Original Trauma

In Genesis it is recorded that God created humankind in His own image, "...in the image of God He created him; male and female He created them" (1:27). Then comes the awesome picture of God forming man from the earth and breathing His own Life into his nostrils. Here was the initial basis of bonding and attachment—Life to life generation. To be sure, there was unfathomable difference between Creator and creature, but in partaking of God's nature we were created as suited for interactive relationship with Him.

Genesis also reveals that there was a break in the parental bond with God. God *entrusted* the care of the earth to Adam and Eve, and they were to *trust* that He, their Creator, would take care of them. Is there any more powerful word in a relationship than *trust?* A relationship without trust is hardly a relationship at all.

One interpretation of God's command not to eat of the tree of the knowledge of good and evil is that God was testing our first human parents to see if they would obey. I believe it could have been a test, but it was also *an opportunity to trust God*. He was telling them what was best for them and letting them know the consequences of not trusting Him.

A *trauma* came by the choice not to trust what God had said. God did not abandon Adam and Eve; they broke the attachment-bond by breaking the covenant of trust. I believe that breaking trust with God was the traumatic blow. The crafty serpent was right: their eyes were opened and they began to know good and evil. However, there was a wicked lie embedded in his words: "...and you will be like God, knowing good and evil" (Genesis 3:5). God knows *good* because He is Goodness, and everything outside of this Goodness is evil. The first humans began to know *good*, but saw it from a distance, from a position of experiencing *evil*, much like broken-off branches looking up at the tree from which they had detached.

At this point, the reality of *sin* enters. Understanding sin and its implications is critical to human healing and transformation. Sin literally means *missing the mark*. The mark is God—everything that He is and all the ways He has hardwired us by creating us in His likeness.

God is Life; He created life on the earth and said all forms of life were good (Genesis 1:31). So, *good* is everything God is, and everything He has created. *Evil*, or sin, is whatever is outside the nature of God. Evil is detachment from Life and has within itself the seeds of death—much as a branch that "decided" to break off from its parent-tree and go it alone. There is death in that decision.

Original Separation Anxiety

Adam and Eve immediately felt the result of stepping outside the relationship with God. They felt *shame* for having broken the covenant of trust; and they felt *fear* because they were separated from the sense of belonging and protection they had with God. There had been an experience of safety in the connection, but now they felt alone and unprotected—in addition to feeling regret for their actions. They were afraid and tried to hide.

In this progression of decisions and consequences, what I call the *Separation Anxiety Disorder of the human race* begins to take shape. It is a trauma that has reverberated down through the ages, becoming so intertwined with human nature as to be a kind of nature in itself—a fallen one.

In Genesis, we basically have a picture of humankind saying, "I'm going to do it my way." After the trust-relationship was broken, they left the Garden of *Eden* (a word meaning harmony and delight—what God intended for us). Out on their own, they and their progeny had to learn to cope with life outside the harmony of their relationship with God. They became *survivors of trauma*, and a difficult and long chapter began for the human race.

It was, and is, a chapter that for centuries has etched upon the earth the development of the human *self*, i.e., the self as existing apart from an intimate relationship with God. Enter *the survivor-self* with its many faces: self-preservation, self-protection, self-confidence, self-reliance, self-respect, and self-image. Enter as well the negatives of self-hatred, low self-esteem, insecurity, anxiety, fear, anger, sadness, despair—and all the searing pain and violence this world has known. But God loves us too much to leave us in such a sorry state.

Assessing the Degree of Human Brokenness

Many do not believe that human nature is fundamentally flawed. Hatred, violence, greed, pain, and anxiety are acknowledged but the conclusion is that it's not that bad...or that we are getting better...or that there is hope if we tap into a deeper wisdom within us and unite as a planet.

In the midst of the evil around us, undoubtedly there is good in the world. God breathed His Life into us and we see evidence of this, like beams of light shining out from the human spirit. Calamities such as earthquakes and hurricanes draw out this light through sacrificial and voluntary acts of service. Various circumstances can call forth bursts of heroism, compassion, and goodness, lighting up what God has planted of Himself in us.

In our daily lives we see evidence of persons seeking and acting on something within—an inner urging that looks to the needs of others, not only oneself. That is the force of love, and is at the very core of being created in God's likeness. The Bible tells us that God is Love. He is also Justice, Forgiveness, Mercy, Wisdom, Goodness, and Truth. We see evidences of all these attributes in the daily course of living as well, but I think of them as so many candles in an enveloping darkness.

Is there a more empirically verifiable reality on this planet than the pervasiveness of human depravity? We experience it every day— within us and around us. For close to 40 years I have witnessed the inner turmoil of normal, everyday folks who have been made crooked and dysfunctional by the abuse or control of others who were intent on having their own way—no matter the cost to others. Then the hurt persons act out *their own afflictions* upon others, often passing them on in the same way. I have yet to meet a person who doesn't have a sack of rocks, each sack loaded with guilt, shame, fear, anger, sadness...and weariness from carrying the load. Some adapt and learn to handle the load, but many stay buried under the weight and decompensate in various ways.

Yet there is something within us that balks at accepting that human afflictions are so deep or extensive. The denial of radical corruption seeps out from a place in our souls where we try to salvage a semblance of self-worth. I lived in such denial for decades and I have seen this phenomenon in many patients. Bookstores have shelves of books devoted to self-worth and self-esteem—how to build self-confidence and develop the power to create your own successful destiny in life. They claim to teach how to overcome all obstacles and become a winner by your own power. "It's within you, just tap into it and pull it out," say the many authors, as if in unison.

However, it's not really difficult to see that things are not getting better. Take a quick look at a comparison of the most prevalent problems in American schools in the 1940s: putting gum on the bottoms of desk seats and running in the halls. Contrast that with today's schools: gang violence, widespread drug use, and bullying that leads to suicides.

Certainly advances in technology have added comforts, more widespread communication, and cures for diseases—leading to longer life spans. But are we better? Are we lessening the gap between rich and poor? Are we eradicating corruption, immorality, and greed? Are we more emotionally and spiritually mature? Are we gaining ground on learning to love one another? Yes we have made technological advances but the same dark side of human nature continues to plague us individually and as a race. In my own therapy practice, the relationship problems that patients bring in are more complex and serious now than 30 years ago.

At the outset of PART II of this book, I want to share the conclusion I have come to, from Scripture and from my life-experiences: I do not believe that we have an innate, intact power-source with which to overcome the darkness, vanquish the violence, and be masters of our souls. Breaking trust with God severed a close-knit bond of fellowship and harmony with Him, the Source of Life.

Like deep-sea divers cut adrift from our air hoses, we have cascaded down through the centuries, generation after generation, passing on the self-centeredness and inclinations to iniquity that develop from living outside fellowship with God. The results of this disconnection are that we have become "poor" (Matthew 5:3); "weak" (2 Corinthians 12:10); "*lost*" (Luke 19:10); "dead in our trespasses"

(Ephesians 2:1); and "thirsty" (John 4:14). We have "gone astray" (Isaiah 53:6) and "don't know the way of peace" (Romans 3:17).

The question I have grappled with in the healing process is: What has the *power* to overcome the entrenched presence of evil and selfishness? I have witnessed anguish, anxiety, pain, and confusion in the hearts of my patients and in my own heart as well. I have also seen and experienced the loneliness, despair, and uncertainty that weigh down and suck the life out of body and soul. These are powerful forces.

A Radical Problem Calls for a Radical Solution

In the Garden, God did not say, "On the day you eat of the tree of the knowledge of good and evil you will have your inner light diminished, and your connection to Me will be strained and stressed. It will be necessary to dig deep inside to find the well of divine life." God said, "...you will surely die" (Genesis 2:17). This means *separated* from God, the only true life-support system. The whole tone of the Garden of Eden Scripture is that mankind would need to be rescued and *resuscitated*. Further, the Bible clearly indicates that the situation warrants *God's* action; the damage is greater than anything humans can accomplish on their own.

For fifty years, in a simple and direct way, Billy Graham has touched the troubled hearts of millions, enabling them to recognize and feel the disconnection, the emptiness, the pain of human life. In his crusades he touches the most tender place of all: *the need to feel loved and accepted*, just as we are. He touches that place with the only words that can heal, i.e., words of love, from the only Person who can confer worth and value—God. "All of us want to be loved," Billy Graham says. "All of us want somebody to love us. Well I want to tell you that God loves you" (in Strobel, 2000). He then goes on to describe that God loves us so much that He gave His Son to take on our sin and wounds, and put us back into relationship with Him, our real Father. Upon hearing this, millions of men, women, and children have opened up their thirsty hearts to drink the Water of Life that quenches the thirst of their parched souls.

These millions have come forward in the crusades when they let the veneer of their self-striving drop, like a mask, and they authentically experienced their true human condition of spiritual poverty and weakness. They acknowledged that they were powerless to change on their own. They realized that they were lost, devoid of real peace, dead and empty inside, and deeply thirsty.

Though I have not attended a live crusade, I count myself as one of the millions who finally let the mask drop. I too felt the disconnection, the separation anxiety, the lack of real power, and the thirst for real life. Like a man dying of thirst, I also drank and found that the Water that really quenches also revives and restores my life to wholeness.

A New Covenant

Immediately after the covenant of trust was broken in the Garden of Eden, God's pursuing, forgiving Love for us is evidenced. He will not leave us nor forsake us. He will deliver us from what we brought upon ourselves. He will bring us back into union with Himself. He promises a Redeemer (Genesis 3:15), a Deliverer who will come out of humankind, fight against Satan and his hordes, and vanquish them.

In Isaiah 53:3-11, the Deliverer is described: "He is despised and rejected by men, a Man of sorrows and acquainted with grief....Surely He has borne our griefs and carried our sorrows...He was bruised for our iniquities...and by His stripes we are healed....My righteous Servant shall justify many, for He shall bear their iniquities."

There is a promise of a new covenant: "Behold, the days are coming, says the Lord, when I will make a new covenant...this is the covenant that I will make...I will put My law in their minds, and write it on their hearts; and I will be their God, and they shall be my people.... For I will forgive their iniquity, and their sin I will remember no more" (Jeremiah 31:31-34).

In ancient Middle Eastern cultures, covenants were blood bonds. Life was considered to be in the blood; blood was used in making life-long commitments. The phrase translated "to make a covenant" in the Old Testament is literally "to cut a covenant." One form of cutting a covenant was the cut made on each palm or wrist of covenant representatives. For example, two tribes would be entering into a covenantal bond with one another, tribe to tribe. The two representatives, one from each tribe, would clasp hands, cut to cut, and hold their hands high. All the members of the tribes could then see the mixed blood running down the representatives' arms, and experience that *all of them* were now bound together in a life-bond and were brothers and sisters.

At the Last Supper, Jesus said that *His blood was the blood of the New Covenant*. As the only sinless man, He could represent humanity— a second Adam, standing in for all mankind, receiving the "cut" as the covenant representative. As God, He was also the divine representative of a new covenant. It was as though, in Jesus, God and man clasped their hands together in the blood bond of the New Covenant. I believe that when Jesus returns to the earth in His glorified state, He will bear the scars in His hands, clearly identifying Him as our covenant representative, our second Adam, the firstborn of new human creation.

As I see it, our disconnection from the original relationship with God became so broken that something as radical as a new covenant had to be established. Only God has the power to effect such a new creation. And He loved us that much. It is clear that He wanted to renew His relationship with us, restoring the Parent/child bond that would allow His love and blessings to pour into us. In Jesus the human branch is restored to its original connection to the God-tree.

At the same Last Supper at which Jesus spoke of Himself as the New Covenant, He also said, "I am the vine, you are the branches" (John 15:5), evoking an image of being grafted into Him by choosing to "abide" in Him, to live in Him. There is an implied organic connection of a branch receiving life-giving sap from the main stem of the grapevine. "I have come that they may have life, and have it to the full" (John 10:10).

This imagery of vine and branches is a core pictorial understanding of the inner healing ministry that I will be presenting in PART III.

Repair or Replace

My journey can be likened to a patient who sought various medicines to salvage his hardened, malfunctioning heart. I said, "It's not that bad; I just need the right treatment; I can get it fixed." Off I went in search of balms, ointments, therapies, exotic exercises, meditation, and every self-help aid I could find. After many denials and attempts to stave off the inevitable diagnosis, I was finally willing to listen to the loving, gentle, yet firm voice of the Physician telling me that I needed a heart transplant and blood transfusion.

I looked into His eyes, saw a depth of Love and Truth that I knew was real, and told Him that I accepted His diagnosis and was willing for Him to perform the operation. I described the surgery in Chapter 4, when God acted on His Word in Ezekiel 36:26: "I will give you a new heart and put a new spirit within you." The spiritual transfusion has been taking place on a daily basis for almost 30 years.

Many years ago, my mother often said "Be a good boy, Billy" as I walked out the door of our house. Decades of my life were spent in frustration as I tried with my self-striving to be good. I pursued this quest in many ways, and then went through seasons of abandoning the pursuit, thinking it futile. But in my last 30 years, *a desire to be good* has awakened from the depths of my soul. I believe that this desire was planted by God. He intends His goodness and holiness to be infused into my character—to make me suited for relationship with Him, and with everyone. I have seen this same desire to be good in patients, colleagues, family, and friends.

In Jesus I have discovered that there is a way to be good. In Him I have become "a new creation," in which "old things have passed away," and "all things have become new" (2 Corinthians 5:17). And by abiding in Him as a branch grafted into a host vine, His Life has been gradually flowing into my soul like an on-going blood transfusion. He has been making me good by replacing my depravity with His goodness. I still have a long way to go.

In the next chapter the immense scope of this replacement-dynamic will be clarified, and the stage will be set for presentation of the ministry of inner healing.

Chapter 10

Reconciliation: The Wellspring of Ministry

The Finished Work of Jesus Christ

As *relationship* was the context for understanding the original breach of trust between humankind and God, *relationship* is also the way to comprehend the redemptive plan of restoring the connection between God and humankind.

In the Gospel of John 19:30, it is recorded that Jesus called out "It is finished!" before bowing His head and giving up His spirit. To be sure, sins were mercifully forgiven and the human sin-nature was dragged to defeat on the Cross that day on a hill called Golgotha. That is the finished work of Jesus. However, there are two other pieces of Scripture that expand the meaning of "finished": "...the Lamb slain from the foundation of the world" (Revelation 13:8), and "...the marriage supper of the Lamb" (Revelation 19:9).

First of all, just as parents have it in their hearts to die, if necessary, so their children might live, God's character is perfect *selfless giving*. He has *always* had it in His heart to do whatever it might take to make it possible for us to have the life-in-Him for which He created us. In that sense, the Lamb of God has *always* been ready to die that we might live; redemption was not some afterthought cooked up when things went awry.

Secondly, God's love extends into the future, to another sense of "finished"...when God's intention of having a vast family of human-divine sons and daughters will be realized...in all that the "marriage supper of the Lamb" connotes. He made us in His image and likeness, so He wants us to be like Him, to have the *same inwrought selfless giving that defines Him* (Fromke, 1998, p. 52). At the Marriage Feast we will be fully transformed—able to relate to Him and to one another with a new capacity for giving and loving.

The finished work of Christ will be finished when these ultimate intentions of God are realized. Redemption is God's story; it is about His ultimate intentions. The whole panorama is about Him, for Him, by Him, and in Him...and especially *in Jesus*.

Notice that all three references are to Jesus: The Cross-principle (selfless giving) of the Lamb slain before the foundation of the world; the historic Cross, "It is finished;" and the marriage feast of the Lamb.

The Ministry of Reconciliation

From the outset it is essential to understand how inner healing ministry is completely within the divine plan of the *finished work* of Jesus Christ. The entirety of the Gospel, and all of the ministries that flow from that Gospel, are contained within the Person of Jesus. As stated in 1 Corinthians 3:11, "For no other foundation can anyone lay than that which is laid, which is Jesus Christ." And all of the thoughts about the finished work of Christ, described above, find succinct expression in 2 Corinthians 5:18: "God...has reconciled us to Himself through Jesus Christ...." Let me carefully unpack the link between the Finished Work of Christ and this "reconciled us to Himself."

Reconciliation is a term of *relationship*. In Matthew 5:23-24, Jesus says that if you have a broken relationship with a brother, go to him and restore harmony before presenting an offering to God. And there is a discussion in 1 Corinthians 7:10ff about reconciliation between husbands and wives. Both of these texts have different forms of the Greek word-group *allasso;* but all forms of *allasso* have the same meaning—*exchange* that is followed by *restoration* (*International Standard Bible Encyclopedia*, 1982).

In a human conflict, two individuals remove obstacles in their relationship by exchanging thoughts, feelings, and understandings— the goal of which is to remove mutual misunderstandings and alienation—replacing them with restoration of fellowship. Exchange is followed by reconciliation.

In 2 Corinthians 5:18-20 we find several forms of *allasso*, with the same meaning: exchange leading to reconciliation...only the process here is *one-sided*, not mutually effected. God is not reconciled; rather,

He reconciles us to Himself. Through the event of Jesus (His death and resurrection) there is a transformation of the relationship between God and humankind.

The amazing exchange that brings reconciliation is the righteous, sinless God-Man taking upon Himself our sins, and pulling down to death our sin-nature, replacing that unholy heap with His righteousness: "For He made Him who knew no sin to be sin for us, that we might become the righteousness of God in Him" (v.20). It was our sin that caused us to be enemies of God (Romans 5:10); the removal of this ground of alienation cleared the way for us to be restored to fellowship with God, i.e., reconciled with Him.

Herein is the radical nature of *exchange*: something is removed and something else is put in its place. In Christ we are changed from enemies to friends. Actually, the exchange is as radical as death and life because separation from God is death—like the image of a branch detaching from its parent-tree—and life is quickened by being grafted back into relationship with God. Our death-dealing alienation from God is absorbed by Jesus and, in exchange, He gives us His Life—making us friends of God. Quite a deal!

The statement "Therefore, if anyone is in Christ, he is a new creation..." (v.17) hearkens back to the first creation. The choices of *trusting God* or *self-independence* are still before us as they were in the Garden of Eden. God has made reconciliation for us, through Christ, and as we choose to receive this reality (the Gospel) and respond to it, we are reconciled (grafted in) to God. It is a personal invitation to step back into fellowship with God: "Therefore we are ambassadors for Christ, as though God were pleading through us: we implore you on Christ's behalf, be reconciled to God" (v.2). This whole process is called "the ministry of reconciliation" (v.18).

Inner Healing and the Reconciliation: A Ministry within *The* Ministry

The American evangelist, D.L. Moody was once walking along a bank of the muddy Chicago River, contemplating how salvation and sanctification work together. Ahead of him he saw a small group gathered in a circle, looking down at the ground. As he approached, he saw a man lying on his stomach in the middle of the group. Someone was kneeling in front of him, pressing on the man's limp body, trying to resuscitate him.

D.L. Moody looked at this man who had just been pulled from the river and saw dirty water running out of his nose, mouth, and ears. Instantly it became a picture of the issue he had been contemplating. In *salvation* a person is pulled from the river of death and his/her spirit-life is saved, quickened, restored. The muddy water that entered a person while he/she was in the river has to be pressed out; this represents the life-long process of *sanctification*. The "dirty water" is expelled from the soul and life-giving "Oxygen" streams in to replace it—the Holy Spirit filling in the vacated places in the soul.

Analogously, I understand my experiences as follows: (1) At Brightmoor Tabernacle in 1984, I had received and responded to the invitation to "be reconciled to God" by a profession of faith in Jesus. The Holy Spirit came to dwell in the innermost sanctuary of my being, i.e., my spirit. I was quickened and enlivened—a new creation. I was pulled from the *river of death. But God did not have all of* me—*not yet.* (2) The first eight chapters give graphic details of *muddy water* that needed to be pressed out of my soul. There were layers of lies, false interpretations of life-experiences, hidden unforgiveness and other sins, and doubts about God's goodness. In addition, I had provided safe harbor for habituated patterns of living by my own wits, self-devised strategies for surviving, self-protective defense mechanisms, victim attitudes of blaming others, and practiced modes of rationalizing, deflecting, detaching, and repressing.

It has taken time and the searching eyes of the Holy Spirit to bring these ways into His Light. Jesus said, "But when He, the Spirit of truth comes, He will guide you into all truth" (John 16:13). As I have already mentioned, a Greek word for truth is *aletheia*, which means *coming from a hidden into an unhidden state.* I had been grafted back into my Creator, regenerated by this Spirit of truth, but the healing and restoration of my soul needs on-going changing out—a continuation of the exchange process of the finished work of the Reconciliation, as depicted in 2 Corinthians 5:18-20.

Along with my spirit, my soul and body had also existed for many years apart from a living connection with God. My soul and body were stuffed with self-centered ways—my soul alienated from God by defiant pride, and my body bound to the earth through unrestrained sensual appetites. All of these ways of the self were not immediately changed out in my soul when I was enlivened by the Holy Spirit. But the way of the Lord was now within me to accomplish the changing out: "...being confident of this very thing, that He who has begun a good work in you will complete it until the day of Jesus Christ" (Philippians 1:6).

The ministry of Reconciliation for the soul-dimension of my being began in 1984 and continues to the present day. The detailed exchanges that took place in me by the inner healing sessions I described in PART I were given to demonstrate how the change-out process works. I now identify this process as *the continuing action of the Holy Spirit in bringing about the fullness of the Reconciliation of Jesus* in me...and in the patients whose stories I told.

I'm sure there is more changing out and exchanging to do but I feel immense peace to be in the dynamic of this Reconciliation, to be in the embrace of the One who has not only taken my spirit onto Himself, but is also the Lover of my soul.

Sin and Wounds.

There has been a mixture of sin and wounds in the muddy water that the Holy Spirit has pressed out of me since 1984, and is still pressing out of me; and I find this same toxic mixture in recipients and patients I have seen over the years. Since Adam and Eve, all generations have participated in the continuous cycles of sin, and the afflictions caused by sin.

As an example, both the sin of the sexual abuser and the deep pain and shame of the sexually abused need cleansing and healing. The First Epistle of John 1:9 tells us that if we confess our *sins* and release them to the Lord, God is "faithful and just to forgive us our sins and to cleanse us from all unrighteousness"—which has already been accomplished by Jesus. And Isaiah 53:4ff tells us that Jesus has also borne our "griefs," our "pain," and our "sorrows"—our *wounds*.

The Call.

Ministers of inner healing are called to be facilitators of a Holy Spirit-led detoxification (sin and wounds) of these muddy waters of souls who come to receive ministry. To be sure, it is God's ministry, fully administered by the Holy Spirit. He alone can extract and dispose of the soul-toxins that we are willing to release to Him; He alone can then pour God's love into our hearts to make us new creatures through and through.

I have accepted the office of being one of the "ambassadors for Christ..." as though God were pleading through me for ministry recipients to "be reconciled to God" (2 Cor. 5:20). I have accepted for myself what God has provided—"the ministry of reconciliation" (v. 18), and have accepted the call to co-labor with the Holy Spirit by facilitating His Inner Healing[4] for others. The place and work of Inner Healing Ministry is the continuation of the Finished Work of the Reconciliation...within the soul.

In a sense, I am a *soul-evangelist*. In ministry sessions people receive the removal of alienation and the restoration of fellowship with God when they, for example, release a lie or doubt about God, and let the Holy Spirit replace that lie with truth about God. Every time a person allows the Holy Spirit to make that kind of exchange in one's soul, God has a little bit more of the person—more of a person's soul has heard and responded to the Gospel of Jesus. Another *enemy*-part has been replaced by a *friend*-part. One is a bit more aligned with God and more synchronized with God's intentions for complete restoration of fellowship with His children—spirit, soul, and body.

The *prayer* of 1 Thessalonians 5:23-24 is a *promise*: "Now may the God of peace Himself sanctify you completely; and may your whole spirit, soul, and body be preserved blameless at the coming of our Lord Jesus Christ. He who calls you is faithful, who also will do it."

---

[4] From this point on, I will capitalize *inner healing* when I mean to signify that I am referring to Christ-realized and Spirit-led ministry and therapy.

The Ultimate Intention of God: a Vision

I end this chapter with a glimpse of what I see as the overarching reality for which the ministry of Reconciliation is intended:

In Heaven, at the Day of Judgment, on the Day of the Lord, at the Marriage Feast of the Lamb, I see many persons fully and gloriously changed out—spirit, soul, and body. The exchange process of the Reconciliation will be complete. All in attendance will be fully healed, made whole, be in the state that God intended from the beginning... holy, undefiled, fully constituted sons and daughters in the family of God. All will be true reflections of His image and likeness. All will be like Christ, glorified in spirit, soul, and body—somehow "married" into Him, within Him, comprising His Body in ways that we cannot now imagine. All will look like Him, as fully illumined lights within His Light—individually different yet alive in Him.

Those at the Banquet will be equipped to be in fellowship with God: communing with Him, worshiping Him, experiencing His Love... and thereby able to love one another, in unimaginably conflict-free, wonderful ways.

I believe this is the Ultimate Intention of our loving God, an intention that is continually and inexorably weaving its way through the tapestry of human lives and throughout God's creation.

> He is the image of the invisible God,
> the firstborn over all creation....
> For it pleased the Father
> that in Him all the fullness should dwell,
> and by Him to reconcile
> all things to Himself...
>
> (Colossians 1:15-20)

PART III

Exchanges for a Lifetime: The Ministry of Inner Healing

Chapter 11

What Inner Healing is Not

1. Inner Healing is not a form of healing that arises out of a *oneness* view of reality.

In the healing processes of New Age-type spiritualities, the task of the therapist, counselor, or coach is to help people make the journey to merge with Universal Consciousness, sometimes called the One. Individuals supposedly dissolve by merging into oneness, into sameness.

The Inner Healing presented in this book is based on a cosmology of real distinction and difference. I look around and see incredible variety in creation. I am often amazed when I recognize someone by facial features or voice and realize that there are billions of people, each one distinctly different. Something deep inside me says that these distinctions are not *maya* (illusion*)* destined to fall away into oblivion when each person sinks into a deep well of a supposed True Self, flowing into the ocean of Universal Consciousness. In Christian cosmology, existence has real distinctions and opposites, divinely written into creation by a Creator.

Further, this Creator is infinite and therefore totally *other* than all he has created. Inner Healing acknowledges God as distinct from His creation, and humans as dependent on this holy God—through worship, obedience, and learning His ways. God has chosen to dwell among us (Immanuel—God with us) in the person of Jesus, but that does not eradicate His otherness and transcendence.

2. Inner Healing is not involved with an impersonal deity.

The God of New Spirituality is an impersonal Force such as Universal Consciousness, The One, The Source, The Whole. This Force supposedly lives in everything, and everything is in this Force.

In Christianity, God is indisputably personal. He offers us relationship, and that is a person-to-person reality. In the Biblical worldview, human beings are unique, individual, real, and are made in God's image and likeness—made to personally relate to God and to one another. Humans are not mere drops of consciousness whose ultimate journey is to shed any sense of individuality and merge into the One.

The Inner Healing of this book preserves and honors the value of *personhood* as an inherent feature of what it means to be created in God's image...a feature designed by Him such that we can be in relationship with Him and with one another—individually and in community.[5]

3. Inner Healing is not solely a transformation of consciousness.

In New Age spirituality, we are sinless, guiltless divine sons and daughters. There is no sense of being fundamentally flawed or in need of a savior. Suffering and evil are due to ignorance of our divinely perfect natures, a condition entirely treatable by learning and applying higher knowledge. Inward transformation of the soul comes to those who awaken to this knowledge and alter their consciousness from "the small mind" (ego, small self) to "the Big Mind" (Higher Consciousness, True Self).

In contrast, Christian transformation does not take place by dropping into or developing a supposed Higher Consciousness or True Self. Because we lost our relational connection to our heavenly Father

---

[5] There is a corporate sense of the Person of Jesus in which the analogy of a physical body is given: "For as the body is one and has many members, but all the members of that one body, being many, are one body, so also is Christ" (1Corinthians 12:12). Here we see the balanced picture of individual members (persons) not living for themselves but having distinct purposes and functions within a collective *whole*. These passages of 1 Corinthians comprise a comprehensive Biblical picture showing that distinctions and individuality exist for a purpose, e.g., eyes or ears serving one's whole body. As Oswald Chambers notes: "The reconciliation of the human race according to His plan means realizing Him not only in our lives individually, but also in our lives collectively....We are not here to develop a spiritual life of our own, or to enjoy a quiet retreat. We are here to have the full realization of Jesus Christ, for the purpose of building His body" (Chambers, 1992).

we need a rescuer, a Savior. Jesus takes away the sins of the world and through Him (a divine Person who also has a human nature) we can be healed and transformed.

Important though meditation and prayer are, and with all due respect to Western mystics and contemplatives, transformation is a change of *identity*. Galatians 4:7 says that in Christ we are no longer slaves to sin but grafted-in sons and daughters. In Romans 5:10, and in other passages already discussed in Chapter 10, it is clear that the Reconciliation is a transformative act that changes humans from enemies to friends of God.

Orthodox Christian mystics have sought a closer experiential intimacy with God *within* the context of a prior conversion experience of becoming a believer in Jesus, not *outside* of that. They do not postulate an *inherent divinity* for everyone no matter what a person believes. Inner Healing stands within this understanding and sees transformation as effected by God through Jesus—now made available in one's life by the power of the Holy Spirit.

Oneness thinking has made its way into various Christian churches and denominations. I just finished reading a book in which a Catholic priest spoke of Jesus as not being an exclusive Son of God, but rather one who points the way to our *inherent divine nature*. He claims that Jesus is just another Son telling us that we too are included as Sons and Daughters. In the author's view, following Jesus primarily means making the transformative journey inward through meditation to discover one's Divinity—a divine inner consciousness that is equated with the Holy Spirit.

In the view of Inner Healing ministry, the above assessment of Jesus and transformation stretches the essential connective tissue of Christian orthodoxy to the breaking point. I do not believe that it is possible to make Jesus into just a teacher or a model and remain within the foundational essence of Biblical Christian faith. Jesus claimed to be the very *exclusive* Son of God—He was put on the cross for blasphemy! The Jewish rulers *got* what He was claiming.

Inner Healing holds to the belief that Jesus Christ is the exclusive, only Son of God, not just an enlightened, awakened, kindred soul who points the way to an altered consciousness called "True Self." Beyond guiding and teaching, Jesus Christ came *to transform* human nature.

4. Inner Healing is not conducted within an undifferentiated moral order.

As described in the first section of this chapter, New Age inner healing moves within an understanding of the spiritual realm as composed of the *same* substance, essence, and being. All spiritual reality is supposedly of the *One* and is therefore *good.* Counselors and coaches direct clients and counselees to "listen to your heart because there you will find your light and truth." In this view there is no sense of sin, flaws, or depravity in human nature. People are led into meditative states and told to find divine guidance or "spirit guides" to help them find their way higher or deeper.

However, as Charles Manson, the hippie murderer from the 1960s, astutely observed: "If God is One, what is bad?" Chilling words, with sobering implications to consider as the doctrine of *oneness* insinuates itself ever more deeply into Western culture.

Biblical Christianity makes distinctions in the spiritual and moral order: good/evil, holy/unholy, God/devil. There are spirits of light (God and angels), and spirits of darkness (Satan and fallen angels). The New Testament is full of references to spiritual warfare (e.g., Ephesians 6) and Jesus talked about evil and the devil more than anyone in the Bible. Inner Healing ministry is completely in accord with this perspective.

The ministry of Reconciliation is all about dealing with evil. Inner Healing is all about releasing the dark side of our flawed nature, and choosing to allow the Holy Spirit to pour in the Light and Life that is the Lord Jesus.

5. Inner Healing does not focus on wounds to the exclusion of dealing with sin.

The Holy Spirit searches out both hidden sin and unresolved emotional pain. The self-drivenness of sin causes wounds and pain when inflicted upon others as well as causing internal damage to the person inflicting the offense.

If those who are afflicted by the sin of others do not receive proper healing for their wounds, they likely will devise survivor-self ways to deal with their pain, ways that often cause affliction to others. On and on, from one generation to the next, the cycle continues. These cycles of sin and wounds have been cascading down all generations of humankind since Adam. On the Cross, Jesus took all sin upon Himself. He also took upon Himself all the sorrow and pain from the sin/wound cycles that afflict all humans (Isaiah 53). We can go to Him for both parts of the cycle. It is a situation of both/and, not either/or.

6. Inner Healing does not stay stuck in the past, instead of dealing with present problems.

If my foot hurts because of a sharp sliver that was embedded there three years ago, that pain is not just a *past* reality dating from the time of insertion. It is also a *present* reality in the pain that keeps shooting from the now-infected foot into my consciousness, affecting my whole state of wellbeing. Not paying attention to the removal of the sliver will keep "the past" stuck in the present. Such is the case when a lie is inserted into the tender soul of a child, e.g., a lie delivered by the words of a father repeating over and over, "you're stupid!" Those words become an implanted soul-sliver and are assimilated as "I am stupid." I have witnessed this internalization many times.

The pain of the sliver is the sense of not measuring up, of being different than everyone else, of being an outsider because "I'm not smart enough." The pain from the "I'm stupid" belief-sliver flares up any time there is a life-incident that calls my intelligence into question. It is a real soul-wound from the past, living in the present. Like a sliver, this lie needs to be extracted and replaced with truth that will heal the wound.

Inner Healing ministry is one way God our Healer can deal with this situation. Until one allows Him to remove such soul-slivers, a person will be burdened with pain and will lack freedom in various areas of life.

7. Inner Healing does not employ the use of hypnosis, hypnotherapy or self-hypnosis.

Hypnosis is a method of bypassing a fully conscious state of awareness in order to persuade a subject to respond to suggestions in a desired way. For example, through the power of suggestion, a hypnotist plants a thought into a person's mind that will cause him to change from having a pleasurable association with smoking to an aversive feeling. Sometimes a trance-like state is induced to increase susceptibility to suggestions.

In Inner Healing procedures, there is no planting of any thoughts, beliefs, images, or suggestions. When a session begins, I request that a person close his or her eyes as a way for the person to focus inwardly on the Lord instead of having eye contact with me. I shift from the role of a counselor to that of a facilitator or assistant. The Holy Spirit is called upon to help the recipient perceive the Lord's Presence and for Him to guide the entire process. Psalm 139:23 NIV indicates this way of proceeding: "Search me, O God, and know my heart; test me and know my anxious thoughts. See if there is any offensive way in me, and lead me in the way everlasting."

No trance-like state is induced. Inner Healing is the opposite of hypnosis which bypasses the conscious state and relaxes a person into a mental state somewhere between waking and sleep. The Inner Healing facilitator encourages a person to be fully awake and aware in order to receive and perceive God's Presence. The expectation is of a person-to-person communication. The process is not suggestion, persuasion, or thought-insertion that bypasses thinking, feeling and willing. The whole person is engaged in Inner Healing.

Also, in hypnotherapy, the therapist can intentionally or inadvertently suggest that certain things might have happened in uncovered memories. The risk of false memories is always present because of the therapist's insertion and control of thoughts, images, and perceptions.

Inner Healing has no such manipulation or suggestion when memories emerge into consciousness. The Holy Spirit brings truth. His whole mission on earth is to bring out truth from hidden places in the soul. The facilitator's role is always to ask what a person is feeling or believing in a memory, or to ask what the Holy Spirit wants a person to know, or what His Truth is. To be free of any suggestive or manipulative mode, questions are asked, answers are not given, suggested, or inserted. The discipline of doing this thoroughly is paramount in facilitating Inner Healing sessions.

8. Inner Healing is not Freudian Abreaction.

Abreaction is a process in psychoanalysis whereby repressed, unpleasant emotions are brought into consciousness in order to be relived and released. Hypnosis is often used as a way to access these repressed experiences. The goal is *catharsis*, a flushing out of repressed, emotional content, as though it were a substance that is contained in a hidden subconscious chamber. What abreaction does not account for is that negative emotions are often symptomatic of festering wounds that need to be healed at the root. For example, embedded lies about one's value and worth can be at the root. Flushing out emotional content may give temporary, symptomatic relief, but the infected wound will fill up with emotion-pus again until the lies are removed.

Inner Healing has healing, not symptom-relief, as its goal. The reason for entering a memory consciously is to let the Lord deal with whatever is there, through His healing Truth. In the process of healing, there may be a release of pent-up pain, but that is released to the Lord as one's Burden-Bearer.

9. Inner Healing is not Jungian Active Imagination

Active imagination is a technique developed by the psychologist Carl Jung. In this procedure, one relaxes into a meditative state and opens up to any images, symbols, feelings, or words that may rise up from the "unconscious" as it tries to communicate with the consciousness of an individual. Whatever bubbles up from the depths is then interpreted by mythology, Eastern mysticism, and other thought systems. Jung instructed his patients to literally drop into the inner world and free-associate with whatever emerged.

Inner Healing calls specifically on the God of the Bible. It is not a meditative process of dropping into a dark, deep pit of the "unconscious." Clearly expressed in the Bible is on-going warfare in the spiritual realm. There are forces of good and forces of evil. There is a Kingdom of Light and a Kingdom of Darkness. It *does make a difference* in what area of the spirit-world one pitches his or her tent. Inner Healing ministry takes its stand on 1 John 1:5, "This is the message which we have heard from Him and declare to you, that God is light and in Him is no darkness at all."

10. Inner Healing is not guided imagery or guided visualization.

Guided imagery is a constructed, visual landscape or scene into which one places oneself, at the direction of a leader. It may be for purposes of relaxation, therapy, or both. Many years ago, when I was part of the New Age Movement, I participated in classes and therapy sessions in which guided visualization was often used as a therapeutic technique. Two of my instructors had trained as Jungian analysts and transpersonal psychologists. An example that comes to mind was one of the instructors leading the class in a guided inner journey. We were instructed to close our eyes and, in our imaginations, create a scene of walking across a meadow and finding a large house. We were then told to go into the house (a symbol of our self) and explore the upper rooms, the rooms on the ground floor, and finally to walk down a long staircase into the dark cellar. Before going down to the cellar we were to find an "inner wizard" or a "wise person," who would help us to find wisdom and understanding.

Who knows from which side of the spiritual spectrum these wizards, wise persons, or spirit guides came? That journey into the spiritual world was presented as though all spirituality was good. We were encouraged to open ourselves to it all. Just jump in. I was naive in those days. It's so alluring to think that everything converges, that *all is one*, that the same good Spirit pervades everything.

In Inner Healing there is no human-guided imagery of any sort. Sessions are Holy Spirit-led from beginning to end. He searches our hearts. He exposes hidden sin and festering wounds. Recipient and facilitator alike follow the guidance of the Holy Spirit. If imagery occurs, that image is not suggested, created, or inserted by human control. We pray for the Holy Spirit to show His perspective, and any imagery that appears is by His initiative.

Chapter 12

Terms of Engagement: the Field of Encounter

Inner Healing is based on an understanding that the place of transformation is the human heart. However, the term heart has myriad meanings. This section begins with the meaning of *heart* that directly relates to the word *Inner* of Inner Healing throughout the rest of PART III.

Field of Encounter: the Heart

Heart (not the physical organ) is descriptive of an integrative, organizing activity within our inner life. It is sometimes broadly distinguished from mind, but throughout various kinds of literature, heart is often connected with the whole complex of what we are passionate about—which involves the mind (thoughts of the heart), as well as the will (intents of the heart).

The heart is a kind of core within the inner realm of spirit and soul. However, it is not helpful to try to contain heart in a static noun, as though it were an object, like the physical heart. *Similar to* the physical heart, the inner heart is a dynamic core of activity.

Passion and attention give direction to the inner heart. As Jesus said, "For where your treasure is, there your heart will be also" (Matthew 6:21). Whatever flows into this inner, organizing center then flows out to the entire organism (much like the pulsating physical heart) through thoughts, words, feelings, and actions. Jesus' words are apt: "For out of the abundance of the heart the mouth speaks" (Matthew 12:34).

Sometimes heart is equated with feelings, but I believe this is a restrictive view. Heart refers more widely to the whole personality and character of a person. Whatever a person treasures flows into this inner core and gradually shapes and expresses one's whole self. A feeling can be a *voice* that expresses what is in the heart but is not to be equated with the heart. If I love someone, that love can radiate outward and find voice in feelings, words, and actions. But the love in my heart is a more comprehensive reality than feelings emanating from that love.

In our culture, we are often told to "Follow your heart," and "Listen to your heart," as though the heart has only good stuff in it. What if laziness and greed are in your heart? What if selfishness rules your heart? What if there is a hidden belief in your heart that ripples outward in an anxious voice that whispers grimly, "You are a loser?"

In describing Inner Healing ministry, *heart* is a significant term that refers to the inner realm of spirit and soul. Where my treasure is (where I put my attention, desire, commitment, time) there is my heart—and where my heart is, in a real sense, there am I.

Perhaps the heart can be viewed as an inner, invisible organ similar to the physical heart. This inner heart collects whatever we pour into our spirits and souls, like the receiving chambers of the physical heart. Then, this inner heart pumps the contents out into the whole organism via thoughts, feelings, desires...all the way out into actions. In this sense, the inner heart is a dynamic repository of deep-seated beliefs, feelings, and motivations. Whatever is there in the heart is like a concentrated essence of one's whole being. To know what is in your heart would be to know *you*.

In Matthew 15:19, Jesus said "For out of the heart proceed evil thoughts, murders, adulteries, fornications, thefts, false witness, blasphemies." When the Holy Spirit comes into a person, He brings into the center of one's personal life, into the heart, the risen Life of Jesus. At that moment the heart-exchange process of sanctification (like toxin-removal and oxygenation in the physical heart) is established to replace wickedness and darkness with Jesus' capacity to love God instead of disrespecting Him, and to love one's neighbor instead of maligning him. This is deep-level change in spirit and soul that is the targeted area of Inner Healing. It is heart-change.

Spirit and Soul

Within the body of believers, there remains a lack of unanimity as to whether spirit and soul are merged together or distinguished in some way. In ministry, questions arise from this ambiguity: What needs healing: the spirit, the soul, or both? What does "Inner" of Inner Healing mean?

Tripartite (three parts) believers often quote 1 Thessalonians 5:23 NIV: "May God Himself, the God of peace, sanctify you through and through. May your whole spirit, soul and body be kept blameless at the coming of the Lord Jesus Christ." Adherents of a dichotomy (two parts) point to the many overlaps of attributes in the Bible. One researcher ended up with four pages of attributes that were ascribed to both spirit and soul (Kylstra, 2001), and resolved the matter by using the term *soul/spirit* for the inner realm.

Hebrews 4:12 is significant: "For the word of God is living and powerful, and sharper than any two-edged sword, piercing even to the division of soul and spirit, and of joints and marrow, and is a discerner of the thoughts and intents of the heart." This would suggest a definite distinction between spirit and soul, but one that can only be discerned by God Himself! Perhaps the image of an *estuary* is fitting: in such a body of mixed water, who can distinguish between ocean water and fresh water? I lean more towards a tripartite view of a distinction between spirit and soul, but the subtle differences are a mystery to me in many ways.

The following is an analogy from Watchman Nee which may shed light (pun intended) on the matter. The image is that of a light bulb:

Within the bulb, which can represent the total man, there are electricity, light and wire. The spirit is like the electricity, the soul the light, and body the wire. Electricity is the cause of the light while light is the effect of electricity. Wire is the material substance for carrying the electricity as well as for manifesting the light. The combination of spirit and body produces soul, that which is unique to man. As electricity, carried by the wire, is expressed in light, so spirit acts upon the soul and the soul, in turn, expresses itself through the body (*The Spiritual Man*, Vol. 1, p. 25).

Lord of the Dance

"And the Lord God formed man of the dust of the ground, and breathed into his nostrils the breath of life; and man became a living being"(Genesis 2:7). This passage suggests a creature that is of the earth (body), enlivened by God's breath (spirit), taking the form of an "ensouled" being. It is a picture of a harmonious interweaving of the parts of human nature.

However, the subject of this book is that the human heart today is not reflective of the smooth-running, harmoniously interrelated organism depicted in Genesis. Human hearts are split apart and riddled with soul-disturbances that find expression in physical maladies as well. We have inherited from our ancestors many of these disturbances and disorders, and then we add to the mess by our own choices. We need healing, restoration, integration, and transformation...and one day that reality will be so.

I end this chapter with an image of spirit, soul, and body learning to move together in harmony and balance, in a coordinated movement demanding integration and synchronization...the image of *dance*. This dance involves our relationships with God, with others, and with everything we are a part of in our daily lives. Sin, pain, fear, shame, anger—all of these can become lodged in our souls and block the flow, disturb coordinated movement on every level, and affect how we walk (dance) through life.

Jesus' heart is to deal with anything that blocks or interferes with the process of becoming one with Him and His Father, because He knows that in this union we will find true integration and wholeness. There is much in the world that tries to divide, block, and interfere with this growth into wholeness. Jesus came as a true and effective Counterforce to the powers that try to do such damage: "The thief does not come except to steal, and to kill, and to destroy. I have come that they may have life, and that they may have it more abundantly" (John 10:10).

I believe there will be music and dancing at the Marriage Supper of the Lamb. The spirits, souls, and bodies of all present will be synchronized and integrated, moving in wonderfully coordinated balance and agility. There will be nothing to block the flow or disturb the dance. Finally, after eons of struggle, human hearts will be whole, not divided. And finally, human hearts will be able to move freely in the dance of fully loving God and one another. There will be much to celebrate. All hearts there will be full of joy and love, just as our joyful, loving Father has always desired and intended.

Chapter 13

Terms of Engagement: Interacting with the Living Word of God

Chapter 12 described the arena of encounters with the Lord—the mysterious interweaving of spirit and soul. The following question will be addressed in this chapter: Within this arena, how can we speak of engaging with God in a conversational way?

The Living Word of God

The second of the Ten Commandments gives a strong warning: "You shall not make for yourself any carved image or any likeness of anything....You shall not bow down to them nor serve them" (Exodus 20:4-5). This admonition and others like it in the Old Testament press us towards an understanding of God as transcendent and invisible. He cannot be *contained* in anything visible, including words and images. In this chapter I will discuss words; in the next chapter I will discuss images.

Jesus said that He would send His Holy Spirit who would personally bring us all truth, and "...whatever He hears He will speak" (John 16:13). However, a problem arises when the process of *bring us all truth* is understood as static, wooden concepts which remain in the intellect and doctrinally *define* rather than vigorously *communicate* spiritual reality. This intellectual approach has greatly influenced the way many view the Bible. In this type of thinking, the Bible becomes a *container*.

In his excellent book, *Hearing God*, Dallas Willard uses the term "Bible Deism" to describe what has happened, especially in fundamentalist religious circles. Classical deism held that God created the world and then went away, leaving humanity to run things—no more intervention in the lives of humans, no miracles. Bible deism similarly holds that God gave us the Bible as a storehouse of truth and then went away, leaving us to figure it out, with no individualized communication either through the words therein or otherwise (Willard, 1999, p. 107).

This is much like the doctrine of the Sadducees in Jesus' time which taught that God stopped speaking after He finished speaking with Moses. Bible deism is the belief that God said all He had to say in the Bible and then stopped speaking—like a manual for a car: go look up the information you need and then apply it. Or like a husband saying to his wife, "I wrote you a love letter before we married. In it I told you I loved you. Go read it."

I believe that the Bible is the written Word of God. It is a written record of the saving truth spoken by the infinite, living God, and, in the words of Dr. Willard, the Bible:

> "...reliably fixes the boundaries of everything He will ever say to humankind. It fixes those boundaries in principle, though it does not provide the detailed communication that God may have with individual believers today....So the Bible is the unique, infallible, written Word of God, but the word of God is not just the Bible....The Bible is not Jesus Christ, who is the living Word" (Willard, pp. 142-43).

The wooden thinking that views the Word of God as totally contained and captured in the pages of a book cannot conceive of the spiritual reality of God *continuing* to transmit personally through the words of the Bible and in direct dialogue. This kind of thinking also does not acknowledge the spiritual *capacity* of believers to receive and perceive, Heart to heart, what God is speaking—the continuing transmission of the living Word speaking into our spirits and souls as we seek Him.

The written words of the Bible are an eminently significant way that divine Presence is *transmitted* to us, Person to person, through the power of the Holy Spirit. His is a *living* Word, not because it's lively, meaningful, and so rich in content. His Word is a living Word because *He is still speaking*. It is not a past tense, done deal. He wants to continue speaking with us. He does continue speaking with us.

When Jesus made a personal connection with my patient Nancy (Chapter 4) via an image of Himself and words of love, the Word of God was *still speaking*. Perfect Love was casting out fear (1 John 4:18). When Jesus told me I was no longer a slave but a son, God was still speaking the words of Galatians 4:7, now to me, in the present moment. When I read Scripture, I first anchor myself by prayer into the presence of the Holy Spirit. I become aware of my relationship with the Lord, and begin to listen to Him and wait on Him to speak to me on this day, in this moment, as I engage with Him.

Words have a spiritual dimension. Words carry thought, emotion, and intention because they are personal forces. Jesus said that His words were spirit and life (John 6:65). He was imparting *Himself* in speaking of eating His flesh and drinking His blood. When God speaks, He doesn't distribute a *part* of Himself; He is *present* with His Word. He *lives* in the Words He has spoken. His Word is Himself in action...as in the Creation—whatever He spoke became a reality...as in His Love—He *is* Love...as in the Word made flesh—Jesus.

Inner Healing is about listening, seeing, perceiving, feeling, and sensing the living Word of God. Unlike Bible deism, biblically-based Inner Healing treats God's communication as mysterious in the sense that it is not possible to contain the living Word of God.

On what basis would we restrict the many ways God may want to speak His Personal Presence into our lives? Why not open up all of our faculties to receive what He has to give? The human mind is a wonderful gift. But, if the intellect is allowed to split off and operate in isolation apart from the rest of our perceptive faculties, we will not be able to receive living reality, only dead thoughts. God speaks Person to person. Why would we want to leave out any dimension or capability of perception that belongs to us as persons?

Inner Healing as Listening Prayer

After enlisting the agreement of a recipient to enter into prayer, an Inner Healing session begins by acknowledging the truth that "...where two or three are gathered together in My name, there am I with them" (Matthew 18:20). I often follow this with a paraphrase of Jesus promising to send the Holy Spirit who will guide us into all truth (John 16:13). Then I ask the Holy Spirit to guide the entire process, to help us discern truth in everything we do during the session. Following this, I request that the Lord help us to perceive His Presence in any way and by any means He chooses.

As we wait on the Lord, the facilitator encourages the recipient to shift into a receiving gear, letting the Lord settle his or her mind into a calm, quiet, expectantly-waiting disposition. If there is not a clear situation for which the person is seeking guidance, I will pray according to Psalm 139 and Jeremiah 17, asking that the Holy Spirit search for and reveal whatever He knows is ripe for healing, for confessing, for burden-relieving, or other ministry. Then we wait on the Lord.

The Hebrew sense of the word *wait* in the words of Psalm 27:14, "Wait on the Lord," is an expectant, faith-filled anticipation of God coming in personal power to bring a good outcome to life's difficulties. It is this disposition of faith and openness to set aside one's own opinions and plans that allows the Holy Spirit to reveal truth.

The process is one of personal interaction with the Word of God, believing, like the centurion with the paralyzed servant in Matthew 8:9, that where there is true authority, there is power. The word is enough: "But only speak the word, and my servant will be healed." Jesus was amazed at the man's faith. He believed and accepted the authority of Jesus, and he walked out his faith in the action of not requiring Jesus to go to his servant's quarters. He asked simply and humbly that Jesus speak the word, and he believed healing would follow. And healing did follow.

I have witnessed many persons, including myself, opening up their inner hearing to the living Word of the Lord, to believe that He still speaks, communicates, heals...that He has indeed not left us as orphans but has sent His Holy Spirit. In Inner Healing ministry, we ask prayerfully that where there is a lie, that He speak His truth; where there is sin to confess, that He is faithful to forgive and cleanse; where there is emotional pain from an invisible wound, that He take that upon Himself and dispose of it; where there is a burden of grief, that He receive that burden onto Himself and bring comfort in its place.

Inner Healing is the prayer of the centurion who stood in the presence of Jesus and pleaded with Him to heal one who was "paralyzed and dreadfully tormented" (v.6). He waited for the Lord's response, and when he saw that the Lord was willing, he opened his heart in faith and expectation, saying, in effect, "Lord, your word is You. Speak, for I know that healing will follow." Lord, increase our faith to that of the centurion.

Conversations with God

Jesus often spoke about listening, and daily spent time conversing with His Father. The conversations were not one-way prayer speeches; He was in dialogue with His Father: "...for all things that I heard from My Father I have made known to you" (John 15:15).

In Paul's conversations with the Lord, three times he begged Him to remove the famous "thorn in the flesh." God was not silent. He responded and said "My grace is sufficient for you, for My strength is made perfect in weakness" (2 Corinthians 12:9). How did God speak to Paul...in an audible voice? By the "still small voice" (1 Kings 19:12)? Perhaps God impressed His thought into Paul's receptive mind? I don't know, but whatever the case, Paul pleaded before the Lord and the Lord responded. As Jesus said, "...how much more will your heavenly Father give the Holy Spirit to those who ask Him!" (Luke 11:13).

Jesus said He would be with us and not leave us, that the Holy Spirit would be with us and live in us. He prayed that we would be one with Him as He is with His Father. These are all relational, whole-person phrases. He did not say He would give us His effects, or His love and wisdom as though they were separate from Him. He gives us Himself. He doesn't parcel out truth like handing out candy to children, or like giving tools to fix cars (though I have seen more than one reference to the Bible as an instruction manual or a set of skills to use).

Jesus, the Word of God, is a Person, not a principle. Truth is a Person—Jesus. The Holy Spirit, who brings us all truth, is a Person. And Jesus is one with the Father, who is a Person. Three Persons, one God, and they are here, Immanuel, God with us...and in us: "...that the love with which You loved Me may be in them, and I in them" (John 17:26).

God is still breathing His Life into us, making us living souls (Genesis 2:7). We live and move and have our being in Him (Acts 17:28). He speaks through the marvelous natural world of His creation. He speaks through images, pictures, and parables. He speaks in the circumstances of our lives. He speaks directly to us in conversations. He speaks as we worship Him individually and corporately. He has never stopped speaking since the beginning: "In the beginning was the Word..." (John 1:1)...and in the *now* is the Word.

I believe God would have us stretch out in faith to meet Him and interact with Him. He wants us to talk with Him and co-labor with Him in many things He is doing on this earth.

Dangerous Waters

Danger lurks in encouraging people to hear from God and to experience His Presence. People can go off the deep end. *Voices* can be one's own inner self-talk, auditory and visual hallucinations from pathologically disturbed minds, or demonic voices that come to us through lying thoughts and perceptions. As whole denominations and churches have plunged into mysticism, New Age spirituality, and wildly charismatic and prophetic streams, a shudder runs through us when we hear the words "God told me." Abject foolishness and devastating tragedy have followed on the heels of those words—witness the utterances of Jim Jones and David Koresh. There are counterfeits, fakery, and confusion. Keen discernment is needed now more than ever.

There is another danger: going off the *shallow* end. This is a more respectable, less wild danger, but as devastating and distorting as the deep end. One day Jesus walked into a synagogue and healed a blind man on the Sabbath. The Jewish leaders, proud of being Moses' disciples, "knew" that Jesus could not possibly be God because working on the Sabbath was clearly not allowed. They "knew" the Bible, and Jesus was clearly a sinner. Even when confronted by the healed blind man, who said "One thing I do know, that though I was blind, now I see" (John 9:25), they rejected the work because it did not conform to their legalistic ideas. They said, "We know that God has spoken to

Moses, but as for this man, we do not know where He comes from" (v. 29).They did not know God in His Love and Mercy even though He was standing there in front of them.

With the same legalistic fervor, many denominations, in reaction to "charismania" or some other wild-side, deep-end danger, restrict the possibility of hearing from God and experiencing God in personal interactions. Of course we must be wary, but there is no scriptural foundation for the total denial of hearing from God.

Having mentioned both ends of the danger-spectrum, let us look at how to go forward into the adventure of discerning God's voice.

Guidelines for Hearing God's Voice and Recognizing His Presence

In the context of Inner Healing ministry, understanding that God continuously speaks is relevant because of the first principle: seeking and waiting on God to manifest His Truth and Presence—listening for Him and Him alone. The most comprehensive guidelines that I have found for accurately discerning God's voice are in Dallas Willard's *Hearing God*. What I am about to present is a distillation of his guidelines and I encourage you to read and digest his whole book. It is biblical, down to earth, and masterfully written.

The still, small voice. Although there have been spectacular experiences of God in visual and audible forms, the most usual and valuable form of individualized communication is the still small voice (1 Kings 19:12), a "gentle whispering" that bears something of the spiritual, unobtrusive stamp of God's personality. "God usually addresses individually those who walk with him in a mature, personal relationship using this inner voice, proclaiming and showing forth the reality of the Kingdom of God as they go" (p. 89).

Discerning the voice. Three factors in the voice help us to discern. These are *quality, spirit*, and *content.*

Quality. The quality of God's voice is more a matter of the weight or impact an impression makes on our consciousness. There is a steady, calm, immediate power in God's voice, without arguing or trying to convince. There is unquestionable authority. Jesus "taught them as one having authority, and not as their scribes" (Matthew 7:20). The Word of God comes with a weight of authority.

Spirit. God's voice speaking within us also manifests a characteristic spirit—a spirit of peacefulness, confidence, joy, and goodwill. It is the spirit of Jesus. It is not a demanding, urgent spirit. Rather it is warm and firm. Our inner freedom-space is not violated; recipients of Inner Healing feel invited, and then they may choose. Rather than feeling driven from behind, as though by a goat-herder, recipients of the Holy Spirit's voice sense that they are being led from the front, as a shepherd would lead.

Content. This refers to the information conveyed. The content of a word that is from God will always conform to and be consistent with the truths about God and His kingdom that are expressed in the Bible. The *principles* of Scripture, not the *incidentals*, count here. Study of the Bible gradually clarifies that certain things are fundamental, absolute, and without exception. Some incidentals have been made principles, such as women having their heads covered. But this is not a teaching that emerges from the *whole of Scripture*.

Some essential principles are the following: God is light and in Him is no darkness (1 John 1:5); loving God with all your heart and your neighbor as yourself (Mark 12:30-31); all have sinned and fall short in God's eyes (Romans 3:23); those who lose their life for Jesus' sake will save their life (Mark 8:35); seek first the Kingdom of God and everything else will follow (Luke 12:31). No specific word that is from God will ever contradict such principles.

Staying close to Jesus. Finally, the key for the accuracy of the three factors of the voice is a life of walking with Jesus on a daily basis. In the opening lines of John's First Letter, there is a graphic expression of John knowing the Word of Life (Jesus): "...which we have heard, which we have seen with our eyes, which we have looked upon, and our hands have handled." It was in the presence of the visible, touchable Jesus that John learned to recognize when God was speaking.

So it is with us through the power of the Holy Spirit. As we rest in Him, we can learn to recognize His voice, His authority, His love, His peace. The Shepherd of the sheep goes ahead of them, and the sheep follow Him because they know His voice (John 10:27).

Even with the existence of dangers and fakery, we in Inner Healing ministry boldly believe that Jesus is the living Word of God who wants to speak transforming Life into all who would come to Him.

Chapter 14

Terms of Engagement: Perceiving with the Heart

The last chapter took up the issue of *hearing* the living Word of God. In this chapter I will focus on *seeing* and *perceiving* through the powerful gift of imagination. What does it mean to see Jesus in one's mind or memory, or to perceive His Presence?

Reclaiming Imagination

Similar to the word inner, imagination has several meanings that cover a wide spectrum—from pure *fantasy*, to a faculty for perceiving *reality*.

On one end of the spectrum, imagination often means imaginary, i.e., unreal fantasy. "You're just imagining that, it's not real." Or it can mean the creative process of conjuring up fanciful images, as in a comic-book illustrator who is spoken of as having a "rich imagination."

In a quest to understand the human faculty of imagination, perhaps even more confusing is the New Age use of *guided imagery* and *active imagination* which I have described in Chapter 11. With both guided imagery and active imagination, there is no control or discernment about the area of the spirit world (region of Light or region of darkness) one may be immersed in through symbols and images.

As with most gifts, imagination can be used for good or evil. Many have distanced themselves from it out of reactionary fear, as Leanne Payne asserts: "Many Christians are not only in denial of their intuitive, imaginative faculties, but are taught to be afraid of them by those in extreme reaction to the New Age and related paganisms" (*Restoring the Christian Soul*, p.179).

On the other end of the spectrum, imagination can be *a way that our mind can independently see and know immaterial reality*. It is a way of perceiving without using either the intellect or the senses. It is a gift from God, giving us access to the spiritual dimension of reality.

Recovering the gift of Spirit-led imagination is critical and was envisioned by A.W. Tozer decades ago:

> A purified and Spirit-controlled imagination is, however, quite another thing, and it is this I have in mind here. I long to see the imagination released from its prison and given to its proper place among the sons of the new creation. What I am trying to describe here is the sacred gift of seeing, the ability to peer beyond the veil and gaze with astonished wonder upon the beauties and mysteries of things holy and eternal (Tozer, 1978, p. 51).

In the context of Inner Healing, the distinction between man-controlled and Spirit-led imagination is vital. Man-controlled imagery uses the imaginative capacity to form and create images or concepts within the mind—ranging from unreal fantasy to reality-evoking poetry. Here, one is *creating* with imaginative power. However, Spirit-led imagery is divinely motivated, using imagination and faith to *receive* communication from Him. This receiving involves the whole person: spirit, soul, and body.

I consider imagination to be a *higher-soul* capacity, a feature of the mind that looks towards the non-material world. As such, it is a multi-faceted power of perception: able to access and apprehend *spiritual* reality, creating mind-pictures and perceptions in the *soul*, and having a location in the brain (right hemisphere) that anchors the process in the *body*.

Jesus is Master in many ways, not the least of which is His mastery of imaginative language.

Jesus' Use of Imagination

A lawyer meets his match. In the Gospel of Luke, an expert in the law stood up to test Jesus and asked Him what he must do to inherit eternal life (Luke 10:25). As the discussion went on, the scholar tried to force Jesus into his narrowly defined theology. Like the Pharisees, these legal experts lived by the *letters* of the texts, not ever trying to understand anything beyond those letters. While Jesus saw into the *spirit* of the law, the scholar could only see the outward law. Though he quoted the law correctly, regarding loving God and loving neighbor, his underlying goal was to trip up Jesus: "But he wanted to justify himself, so he asked Jesus, 'And who is my neighbor?'"

Immediately Jesus used the imaginative part of His mind to cut through the intellect-snare set by the lawyer and go directly to his heart. This is a paraphrase, but He might as well have said, "I want you to picture a man going down from Jerusalem to Jericho..." (Luke 10:30). Then He unfolded the story of the Good Samaritan and we have, still speaking to us today, the Kingdom of God's powerful "definition" of *neighbor*. The pictorial story does not give concepts and principles to file away in intellects; it conveys the loving-character of God right into *hearts*. As such, the story does something that no intellectual concept can do—be a *vehicle* of invisible reality, carrying it directly into the inner person.

Scripture records no reply to the parable by the lawyer. No doubt he was speechless. Jesus gave an answer that flooded the lawyer's intellect, pouring powerfully over his whole mind and directly into his heart and soul. And to make sure the *will* was touched, Jesus said, "Go and do likewise."

The parables. Next, consider how Jesus conveyed the principles and truth of His Kingdom. I paraphrase: "What is the kingdom of heaven? Let Me show you. Imagine a man planting a tiny mustard seed in his field and, when grown, the seed becomes a large tree with birds in it....Picture a woman hiding some yeast in a batch of dough and then it rises and expands....Imagine a man finding a treasure in a field. He joyfully sells all that he has and buys the field in order to obtain the treasure" (Matthew 13:31-46).

Can you experience how and where these images touch you? I invite you to feel how they touch the places in your heart where you seek truth, where you want to know true value in life, where you determine what is important in life. Soul-searching questions arise: What are you willing to give up for such great treasure? Are you willing to sell everything in order to obtain it?

In these images, Jesus communicated spiritual truth that hearers received through their imaginative capacities. And He is still speaking those truths to us today as we take these images into our souls. The images are not meant to be dead concepts that collect cobwebs in our minds; these images convey spirit and life.

Eating and drinking. In one of the most powerful passages in Scripture (John 6:53-56 NIV), Jesus used imagery to express a deep truth, one that He wanted His hearers to receive in a *literal* way in their spirits and souls.

I tell you the truth, unless you eat the flesh of the Son of Man and drink His blood, you have no life in you. Whoever eats My flesh and drinks My blood has eternal life, and I will raise him up at the last day. For My flesh is real food and My blood is real drink. Whoever eats My flesh and drinks My blood remains in Me, and I in him.

On the natural plane, when we eat food and drink, they are absorbed, assimilated, and eventually transformed to become *life* in every cell in our bodies. Jesus uses this image to make it clear that He offers to be in us in a real way. The image conveys the spiritual reality of Him in personal union with us.

Note that the image of eating His flesh and drinking His blood is not a metaphor to express anything fanciful or a dramatic way to express an idea. Jesus said, "The words that I speak to you are spirit, and they are life" (John 6:63). On the physical plane, flesh and blood comprise the entire body. Blood especially is seen as the carrier of life. On the spiritual plane, flesh and blood mean His whole Self, His Life. It is an image of personal intimacy and union: "He who eats My flesh and drinks My blood, remains in Me, and I in him" (v. 56).

What does it mean spiritually to eat Jesus' flesh and drink His blood? It suggests a process that is personal, whole-hearted, and full of life-altering import. Hearers and readers can reject the image as a strange, cannibalistic-sounding metaphor. Or, it is possible to codify it into a lifeless concept "intended" by Jesus for us to take our relationship with Him seriously. Or lastly, we can let the image speak the spirit and life that Jesus said it did, receiving it via our imaginative abilities into the inner recesses of our souls.

In doing the latter, we will confirm that true belief in Jesus is much more than a *mental assent* to the existence and truth of Christ. True belief is transformative, as attested to by Paul in Galatians, 2:20: "It is no longer I who live, but Christ lives in me."

Similar to the Good Samaritan parable, I believe Jesus intended us to receive His words through imaginative perception so that He could impart living, dynamic truth into our hearts. Certainly He meant to speak to our minds, but it was Person to person communication. Such communication touches our consciences, emotions, values, spirits—everything that makes up who we are as persons. Just as physical food and drink nourish every cell in a human body, eating and drinking the spiritual flesh and blood of the Lord restores every "cell" in our souls.

These passages and parables illumine the ministry of Inner Healing. I will show this process in some of the Inner Healing sessions already described.

Imaginative Language and Spiritual Presence in Inner Healing Ministry

Nancy's Inner Healing sessions. The separation-anxiety that Nancy suffered for 42 years was dispelled by Jesus communicating His Presence and Love through the image of a visual picture of Himself (Chapter 4). Nancy recognized the presence of Jesus in this picture within her memory. By faith she opened herself to let the Lord express His love and protection through imaginative imagery, and she was willing to receive it.

When Nancy saw Jesus standing next to her bed in the memory-picture from her life at age five, the Person of Jesus by the power of the Holy Spirit was communicating with her in the sphere of her spirit and soul. It was relational presence, from Jesus to Nancy, and it was Real Presence, i.e., He was somehow really there. Jesus said in John 16:12-14, "I still have many things to say to you...when He, the Spirit of truth, has come, He will guide you into all truth...whatever He hears He will speak; and He will tell you things to come...He will take of what is Mine and declare it to you."

However, the picture of Him in the memory mediated and *conveyed* His Presence to her, but the picture did not *contain* Jesus. Jesus was truly present to Nancy through the power of the Holy Spirit; yet the reality of Jesus currently sitting on the Throne in His ascended glory is also true in any given moment, according to the witness of the Word (Colossians 3:1 and Hebrews 12:2). Mystery and Truth co-exist here.

When Nancy sensed and received the Holy Spirit into her past and present, she felt a peace-filled connection to her life. Fear and anxiety had uprooted her security and peace from childhood. At last, the free-floating anxiety was quieted by God's Spirit acting within Nancy's spirit and soul. The words of Zephaniah became true for Nancy: "He will take great delight in you, He will quiet you with His love..." (Zephaniah 3:17 NIV).

My Inner Healing sessions. In Chapters 3 and 4, I described three images through which Life and Presence were transmitted into my being:

1. Vine and branch. When I heard the Lord speak the words "I am life" to me as I stood in a pew in Brightmoor Tabernacle, and I said "yes" to His invitation, something happened in that moment. And in the ensuing weeks when I made an informed profession of faith and demonstrated it publicly by baptism, a spiritual grafting took place. Another human, broken-off branch was grafted back into the Vine by the Holy Spirit. Life-giving, spiritual Sap of the Vine began flowing from my spirit into my soul. I literally became a re-attached branch spiritually, but there were obstacles in my soul that needed clearing away and changing out so the Sap could flow more freely.

2. A stony heart. After leaving the seminary, I gradually turned away from God and turned toward self, drugs, and sensual living. I developed a survivor-self...pulling into myself defensively and trying to medicate my pain and anger. I hardened up, becoming vigilant against suffering further pain. I became an island unto myself—cut off from the nurturance and life that comes from relating to others or to God. Self-enclosed hardening set in.

Bereft of spiritual or relational nurturance, and weakened by the numbing effects of drugs, my heart had slowly formed into what would be called on the natural plane an inorganic substance—like a *stone*. Radical soul-surgery was necessary.

I pleaded with God for this surgery: "I will remove from you your heart of stone and give you a heart of flesh. And I will put My Spirit in you..." (Ezekiel 36:25-27 NIV). Through His living Word in Galatians 4:7, God shattered my heart-encasement and spoke His Truth: "You are no longer a slave but a son." As I received this truth, it set me free and I allowed Him to remove my heart of stone and replace it with a new heart...into which His Spirit could flow.

Through the imaginative capability in my soul, along with faith, I perceived and received Truth, Life, and the very Presence and Power of God. For me, Ezekiel 36:25-27 is not a nice-sounding metaphor. God shattered and surgically removed my heart of stone. He replaced it with a heart of His re-creating, into which I could receive the living truth that I am His son. My life has not been the same since that surgery.

3. The parable of the lost son. The parable of the lost son and my life-story are still fused as I write these words. I continue to feel the relief and joy I first felt years ago when experiencing my Father running out to meet me. The loving Presence of my Father and His words to me, His son, are still conveyed to me through the medium of the story.

I thank God for His awesome gift of imagination; to me it is another way that He demonstrates how much He desires to reach into human lives and gather us to Himself.

Chapter 15

General Guidelines for Facilitators

To Begin: God-Consciousness

In Inner Healing, the replacement-process of sanctification is one in which the recipient grows into *what God intends*, so facilitators begin each session in prayer, calling on His guidance from the beginning. We begin with *God-consciousness*, not *self-consciousness*. When reconnected to that inner place of communion with God, through becoming spiritually grafted into God as sons and daughters, we can begin to inquire of the Lord, listening and speaking with the Lord in quiet conversation.

The whole process is about God's plans and His intentions. A deadly *me-thinking* has crept into Christian culture, cloaked in religious language and Bible quotes. In this self-centered view, "sanctification" becomes the realization of my whims and desires, so I can meet my goals—as found in prosperity and personal-growth models. In these models God is seen as a kind of celestial errand boy, here to serve us. This is inverted "Christianity" whereby humans become masters and God is the servant.

In an Inner Healing session, after connecting with the Lord in prayer, what initiates the soul-search in a recipient is not a seemingly obvious trauma or painful incident that may stand out from hearing a person's biography. We call on the Holy Spirit to select: "Search me, O God, and know my heart...see if there is any wicked way in me" (Psalm 139:23). "Any wicked way" might be a recipient's sin, or it might be a wicked act that was done to the recipient, resulting in trauma, abuse, or another kind of affliction. The primacy of the Holy Spirit over mind-analysis is a paramount first principle: "I, the Lord, search the heart" (Jeremiah 17:10).

In Revelation 3:20, Jesus says "Behold, I stand at the door and knock. If anyone hears My voice and opens the door, I will come in to him and dine with him, and he with Me." I know that there are various interpretations of this passage, but for us in Isaiah 61 Ministry, the image evoked is a depiction of this first principle of seeking the Lord and His guidance.

When a memory or an incident in a recipient's life comes onto center stage of consciousness, we *invite* Jesus to be with us in that place. Jesus says He will "dine with him," i.e., bring the Bread of Life and the Water of Life—Himself—to minister to the person. In Him and with Him (the true Temple of God) the way is open to have the Life of the Holy Spirit in a person's innermost sanctuary (spirit) flow into his or her inner court (soul). And then the soul-exchanges take place. The last line of the passage even suggests the action of an exchange: "I will come in and eat with him, and he with me."

We do not conjure up anything, or "bring Jesus" into a picture or memory, or ask Him to do some action that *we think* would be beneficial. We ask what ministry He wants to bring this day. Again, we believe that the Holy Spirit is here not for our whims or demands, but here to administer God's intentions. As a facilitator, one is simply to ask the Holy Spirit to manifest how He wants to continue applying the finished work of Jesus Christ in His Reconciliation...in this moment, on this day, in this ministry session, for this willing recipient. We come before the Lord humbly, seeking Him, inviting Him, and surrendering to Him and to His guidance, every step of the way.

Not a Counselor

A counselor is an advisor, a strategist, an analyzer, and a problem solver. A Christian counselor is expected to be a biblical scholar and one who knows how to apply truths and principles found in the Bible and elsewhere.

I will speak more fully about the differences between Inner Healing and counseling in Chapter 20, but a main difference between being a counselor and a facilitator is the person sitting in the driver's seat in each process.

For years I was a Christian counselor firmly sitting in my pilot's chair, asking God, my co-pilot, to get us off the ground when beginning a session (opening prayer) and asking Him to bring us in for a smooth landing at the end.[6] It never dawned on me that the injunction "If we live in the Spirit, let us also walk in the Spirit" (Galatians 5:25) might pertain to *walking through a counseling session* in the Spirit, as well as through every activity in life.

Inner Healing acknowledges that mostly it is God who is working during the ministry session. God's heart and character are to heal. Jehovah Rapha, the God who heals (Exodus 15:26), is one of His names. "Rapha" means to *mend*, as in mending a torn cloth. The word connotes curing, healing, repairing, restoring, making whole again. People come for help because they are ravaged by sin and emotional pain. They need Real healing and Real transformation deep in their hearts—more than they need insight, advice, and strategies for stress-reduction.

It is God who "heals the brokenhearted and binds up their wounds" (Psalm 147:3); it is the Lord who is "near to the brokenhearted and saves the crushed spirit" (Psalm 34:18 NASB). He is the Physician, the Surgeon, and the Counselor. The Lord has the compassion, the interest, and the *power* to heal. When I switched into the co-pilot's seat and began to facilitate direct encounters between a person and the Lord, His power and wisdom flowed into ministry sessions in unmistakable and effective ways.

His Beauty for Our Ashes: Facilitating the Exchange

Living and walking in the Spirit also means listening in the Spirit. I spend much of my time during an Inner Healing session in a quiet interior dialogue of prayer with the Counselor—asking, listening, receiving, and moving with Him from step to step. Almost invariably, I find that the meanderings in and out of incidents and memories end up in a specific "deal" that the Lord has in mind for the recipient.

In the Exchanges Diagram below, I have depicted the interchanges of Inner Healing sessions. As facilitator I stay attuned to the Holy Spirit

---

[6] Several years ago I actually pulled up behind a car with a bumper-sticker that read: "If God is your co-pilot, switch seats." In a phrase, this describes the role-shift for facilitating Inner Healing ministry.

and wait for the invitation of the Lord to emerge in the dialogue. Lies, fear, shame, and sorrow will emerge from the shadows of the soul into the light. When this happens the minister's role is to clarify the "business" that the Lord wants to conduct, and to serve as an intermediary. One is still an assistant, but also a coach[7], pointing out what is targeted to be released, if the recipient is not able to discern clearly what is ready for exchange.

For example, an independent, self-sufficient part of a person emerges in a memory along with an embedded belief that *I have to take care of myself because no one else will*. When held up to the Lord in direct dialogue, the recipient senses or hears or receives an impression that the Lord is saying "I will take care of you." Then the facilitator puts on his coach's hat and asks the person what he or she wants to do with what has been heard/realized/sensed. That old belief was placed there by choice and will be removed when a person is willing to give up the belief and receive the perspective that the Holy Spirit offers.

In the list of words under RELEASE in the diagram, I have listed just some of the many manifestations of our sin-nature that Jesus pulled down into death. Part of the coaching of a facilitator is to point out the recipient's option to release ungodly beliefs, shame, and other forms of darkness to the Lord Jesus. The Cross is a living symbol. Mysteriously the Cross signifies Jesus drawing all wounds, curses, and sins unto Himself, for disposal.

The horizontal infinity sign in the diagram depicts the exchange-process within an Inner Healing session: As a recipient releases, e.g., *shame,* to the Lord Jesus, the minister then facilitates the rest of the exchange—a recipient RECEIVES the inflowing truth and love of the Holy Spirit. In the case of shame, a person might receive some form of acceptance, worth, or cleansing as a replacement.

---

[7] A case could be made for Inner Healing being more closely identified with coaching than counseling.

Exchanges with the Master
The Ministry of Reconciliation

"God was in Christ
Reconciling the world
to Himself."
2 Cor.5:19

RELEASE	RECEIVE
sin	forgiveness
unrighteousness	righteousness
affliction	healing
brokenhearted	whole hearted
imprisoned	freedom
sorrow	joy
lies	truth
evil	goodness
darkness	light
hatred	love
pain	comfort
fear	peace
separation	belonging
shame	delight
rejected	accepted
self-sufficiency	God's sufficiency
guilt	debt-free
cursed	blessed
despair	hope
defeated	victorious
far off	made near
enemy	friend
death	life

In the Diagram, all three Persons of the Godhead comprise the living context of the actual exchange: the heart of the *Father's* love suffuses the whole scene...love which is brought into our midst by *Jesus* through the Cross...and then Jesus' risen Life is distributed into the time and space of our lives by the *Holy Spirit,* symbolized by the Dove.

The invitation that occurs within an Inner Healing session is actually an invitation into the restorative exchanges of the Reconciliation of 2 Corinthians 5:18. Sanctification means the Holy Spirit forming Christ's nature into a person—literally "Christ in you" (Colossians 1:27). That's why this book has *Exchanges with the Master* in its title. Inner Healing is about changing out the old, corrupted, dragged-onto-death, Adamic nature, and letting the Holy Spirit replace the old with the new...the New Adam Himself. "New" means *His* life, *His* holiness, *His* love, *His* purity. The Christian life is an ongoing *impartation* of Jesus, not an *imitation* of Him.

Listening for Alignment Issues

The Lord's primary focus is on the *alignment of a person's heart with His heart*. When synchronization with Him takes place in the heart, then a person has the inner resources to deal with any situation.

Within listening for the invitation of the Lord, it is important to become aware of the alignment issues that are often at the center of the turmoil in a recipient's life. No matter the context (individual, marital, relationship, work) the underlying issue often involves a patient's relationship with God. For example, *fear* is a perception of being alone, with no one present to keep a person from harm. *Shame* wants to hide and believes its place is in outer darkness. *Guilt* speaks of owing a debt and generates feelings of unworthiness. *Anxiety* is doubt that God is in control and cares for me.

All of these beliefs carry doubts about God, anger at Him, mistrust of Him, and perceived relational distance from Him. In the perceived absence of a good and loving God, *self* willingly and eagerly ascends to the throne of the soul.

So many times, in my own life and in the lives of others, I have seen the fog drift away in an Inner Healing session, and the clear resolution that the Lord has in mind comes into focus, revealing some aspect of one's *misalignment with Him*. He delights in us dwelling in Him more closely, and He knows that we function in life better when we live as He designed us—dependent on Him and trusting Him in all circumstances.

Attunement: the Power of the Lord's Presence

After many years in the field of mental health, it is my belief that much of *feeling better* after emerging from a counseling session is due to relational attunement. This means that a compassionate and understanding person is present with another person. A therapist usually listens well and establishes relational connection with a client. This connection feels better than being alone.

Many presenting problems carry a painful, anxiety-provoking state of aloneness—rejection, shame, abandonment, feeling like a loser, an outcast, unworthy. When a counselor is visibly and emotionally present with a person and his pain, the relational connection and words of compassionate understanding temporarily diminish the pain. But a human presence such as a counselor's does not have the *power* to resolve deep-seated beliefs of being alone or feeling unprotected and unworthy.

Remember Nancy's story in Chapter 4? The presence of Jesus in her memory as a four-year-old changed everything for her. He who said "I am the Truth" let her know that He had always been there watching over her, and He always would be there. His Presence dissolved the darkness of feeling abandoned, and it cast out her fear. She experienced the Lord delighting in her and having an interest in being with her. The attunement of this Presence had Real power and the healing effects in her lasted.

I have seen the simple reality of the Lord's Presence convey numerous healing truths, wordlessly. His Presence says the following: God cares; He is providing for me and protecting me; I must be worth something if He is here with me; I'm not alone and I'm not an outcast...all of which realizations exude peace, comfort, and a sense of belonging.

Sometimes the best role for a facilitator is to make sure that a recipient stays connected to the Lord and retains a sense of His Presence. During a session, periodically drawing a person's attention back to the God-consciousness with which the session began is a good way to assure that relational attunement with the Lord is maintained.

Committed to One's Own Healing

Years ago I was part of a Christian counselors' fellowship. One day we were discussing how counselors need to continue pursuing their own healing in order to be effective with patients. A Christian psychiatrist spoke up to say that in his training he had gone through psychoanalysis and did not need anything more; he was finished with his healing. Unfortunately this is not an uncommon view. I too succumbed to the shortsighted idea that my academic training provided most of what I needed to be a qualified counselor. Now, after more than a dozen Inner Healing sessions, I realize what a landfill of lies and soul-sludge is layered into my soul.

It takes courage for a recipient or patient to enter painful places in the soul. A facilitator needs to have had that same courage and to know from his own healing that the Lord will be there, and that He desires to bring truth and peace.

Chapter 16

Exchanges with the Master: Steps in the Ministry of Inner Healing

This chapter will be relatively brief. Although these steps basically represent what our team members use in Isaiah 61 ministry sessions, they are steps I have adapted from my training under the tutelage of the Holy Spirit. They are guidelines, not meant as recipe-steps of a formula. When I train Inner Healing ministers, I use the basic structure within these steps; but I have noticed that when anyone surrenders to the Lord for this service, the Holy Spirit fine tunes each person according to how He wants to use the person. Our team believes that as a team we are anointed for ministry, and within this anointing there are diverse expressions. There are many members, all different, in the body of Christ.

This chapter will also be brief because, although intended to be a training guide, this book is not meant to be an exhaustive manual that takes the reader through the many complex issues which can arise in an Inner Healing session. For example: obstacles to the process when a recipient is resistant, blocked, numbed, or otherwise shut down; how to deal with anger at God; steps in the forgiveness process; what to do when a recipient doesn't sense the presence of God in any way...and various other difficulties. These are important issues that warrant special treatment, and in the AFTERSTORY I direct you to several resources I have drawn from, in case you are interested in learning how to navigate in unpredictable waters.

1. Beginning the Session

I start off in a counselor-role as we review situations in daily life in which the person experiences a lack of peace—anxiety, anger, shame, etc. As a preparation for an Inner Healing session, I sometimes suggest observing occurrences in which one feels a $500 internal reaction to a

$5 offense (e.g., feeling profound pain at an acquaintance's dismissive tone). This is usually a good way to begin unearthing and opening the channels to the hidden reservoirs of pain in one's life.

Whatever might be unearthed through a review of symptoms, incidents, or known traumas, the signal that one is ready for an Inner Healing session is not so much what is unearthed in a life-review; rather, the sign of readiness is in the expressed *willingness* to give all over to the guidance of the Holy Spirit and to listen for His direction.

I then take a moment to make a clear role-shift, indicating to my patient that I will be assisting and facilitating an encounter between him and the Lord. I ask the recipient to close his eyes as I break eye-contact with him and invite him to open his inner eyes and ears. Out loud I acknowledge the Presence of Jesus through the power of the Holy Spirit, asking the Lord to help the recipient perceive His Presence in whatever way He chooses.

While the patient is quietly allowing God-consciousness to replace self-consciousness, I am silently asking the Holy Spirit to attune and align my heart with His, that He will clear my mind and focus my attention on the interaction at hand. When the Inner Healing process begins, I am in the theatre of the Master Surgeon as an obedient assistant, helping Him accomplish His intentions. The Lord is the Real Caregiver. I am one of the men (Mark 2: 4) lowering a paralytic down through the roof, into the presence of Jesus, so He can touch and heal him.

2. Inquiring of the Lord

Aloud I ask the Holy Spirit to bring to the recipient's mind a beginning place for the ministry He intends for this person on this day. Usually the first thing that comes to a patient's mind after this prayer is where I begin to inquire of the Lord, acknowledging His Presence with us, asking Him to highlight whatever He is after. I find it important to *refresh* a sense of the Lord's Presence from time to time during the session, making sure the patient in some way feels or is aware of His Presence with us.

Staying connected to the Lord is especially important if the memory selected for the day is a severe trauma. A previously-mentioned image is that of a child being afraid to go into a dark cellar alone, but he will descend the stairs if his father holds his hand. The Presence of Jesus can give a recipient the courage and the capacity to enter painful or fearful memories.

At this point, as a facilitator and assistant, I am fully engaged in listening to the Holy Spirit, asking for His direction and guidance, and following His lead.

3. The Exchange Process

a. Tracking beliefs. When it is clear what the Holy Spirit intends and where He wants to begin, I begin asking the questions that I have learned are of assistance in anchoring a patient into a memory. Initial questions elicit the details of the physical surroundings, the people involved, the age of the person at the time of the memory...gradually moving within the memory to bring out a story that might never have been told: the story of what the recipient (perhaps as a child) was feeling, thinking, and believing at the time. That information is recorded in the memory—sometimes easy to extract, sometimes difficult, but the information is there.

Usually *feelings* are the best tracking device to get to beliefs and interpretations that one made at the time of an incident. For instance, if a patient remembers being a child in a situation that takes place shortly after her parents have divorced and she is feeling guilt in that memory, a question such as, "Why are you feeling guilt there?" might surface an internalized belief: *I caused the divorce because I misbehaved too much.*

Sometimes the *actions* in one's current life are a tracking device the Holy Spirit can use. I once had a patient who had just lost his wife through divorce and was about to lose his third career. He was desperate to know why he kept sabotaging every endeavor in his life. As we prayed for the Holy Spirit to show him the true answer to his desperate plea, a long-forgotten memory popped into his mind.

In the memory he was in his high school's state wrestling tournament, up against the reigning champion in his weight class. He had become an excellent wrestler by staying long hours after school to practice so he wouldn't have to return home to his critical father—who repeatedly yelled at him that *he would never amount to anything.* During the wrestling match, in the semi-finals of the tournament, my patient described how he had a winning hold on his opponent. But just before he flipped and pinned him, an image came into his mind of being the next state champion. Inside, his internalized belief that *he was a loser* caused him to startle at the discordant sensation of being a winner. He loosened his hold for a moment. His opponent slipped out of the hold and proceeded to flip and pin him—winning the match.

This memory unfolded in his mind's eye in response to his desire and prayer to know why he behaved like a loser in his adult life. He had never made this connection and was amazed at what the Holy Spirit showed him. He opened his eyes and tears began to fill them. He looked at me and said, "That is the story of my life."

b. Resistance. Often I have to negotiate with a protective layer of personality that forms in the soul as a result of injury, especially if there has been severe trauma. Through my own Inner Healing I have come to respect this protective part of a patient, even if it manifests through anger, denial, avoidance, and a tendency to isolate. If I am going to assist the Holy Spirit in gaining access to painful regions of the soul I need to build trust with this protective part that does not easily allow access to hidden reservoirs of pain.

Walls and fences in the soul are there for a reason, and are there out of previous choices that were made. Likely they will be removed by choice, and when it is safe to do so. I am still in the role of an assistant here, building trust so that the protective part may be willing to participate in the interactive process. I have found that the Lord is amazingly gentle and wise in dealing with all the split-off parts of our souls.

c. Clarifying what is to be released. I keep my heart attuned to the Spirit, waiting for His prompting to see the invitation—what He is pointing to in a person's soul that is ripe for release onto Him and the Cross. Slowly but surely, rising out of the memory, are the ashes to be exchanged for His beauty: the sin or affliction that is to be reckoned as fixed upon the Cross, the lie that is to be released...to be replaced by Jesus' risen Life and His Truth.

At this point I become a coach, clarifying for the patient what is to be released, and encouraging the person to make the release, if he or she is willing. The willingness is crucial, and I usually have the recipient respond to the invitation out loud so I can witness it and make sure that a deed is taking place, not just an uncommitted thought. "I want to release this lie to the Lord" is a step removed from "I release this lie to You, Lord." Coaching is helpful, but if a person is unwilling to give over the ashes of unforgiveness, shame, or a lie, then an exchange can't take place—at least not on that day. *Exchange* is a radical word: something has to be given up before the replacing-reality can fill the vacated soul-space!

If a person is to release a sin through confession, then the exchange is to receive forgiveness in the place of the sin. If the recipient is to release a deep sorrow or a trauma-pain, then I will facilitate an exchange in which a person releases that pain, and then I pray for the Holy Spirit to fill the place from which there was release. But when there is a lie or a false interpretation of a life-experience that has emerged, I usually immediately pray that the Lord show the person what He wants him or her to know from His perspective: "Lord Jesus, what is Your Truth?"

When the Lord shows what is in His heart, in whatever way He chooses to express His Truth, then I ask recipients if they are willing to release the old and to receive the new: *It is a moment to choose to step into the Reconciliation (2 Corinthians 5:18) and let the Lord continue restoring creation to His Father.*

d. Release and receive. If the recipient chooses to release and to receive, I encourage *full* release by coaching the person: "release... release...flowing out...let it go to the Lord." When the release is finished, I encourage the recipient to shift into receiving-mode and I begin to pray for the second half of the release/receive interaction: receiving Christ's Life by the ministry of the Holy Spirit. I coach: "Filling...filling...receiving...let the Lord pour in His Life, Light, Truth... however and whatever He chooses." I encourage the recipient to receive and allow the Holy Spirit to fill the soul-space vacated by the release: Life for death, Light for darkness, Love for fear, Truth for lies. Often I witness delight replacing shame, acceptance replacing abandonment, and peace replacing turmoil. It is the work of the Holy Spirit to accomplish the exchange, and He does so time after time when recipients release and then receive of His Goodness.

In the two examples given above, my first patient was willing to release the lie that *it was her fault that her parents divorced*. The Lord showed her His truth that what happened with her parents was between them, and that He was involved with them in the whole situation of their conflicted lives. She released the guilt and received a wonderful sense of peace as the burden of this misinterpreted sense of responsibility was totally removed from her soul.

My second patient, the wrestler, opened his soul to the Lord who poured forth profound words of affirmation, love, and worth. The man let the Holy Spirit do a thorough exchange as he renounced and released the lie of being a loser, followed by a realization streaming into his mind that *His real Father thought of him as a winner*. The lie of being a loser had been deeply embedded, and it took more than one session before he was willing to release this belief and forgive his father. But once he did, he wept tears of joy and relief as much as he had wept tears of pain and despair in our first session.

4. Ending the Session

After the ministry-transaction seems to be complete, I ask aloud: "Lord, is there anything else You want 'George' to know from the ministry that You did today?" If the direct dialogue with the Lord seems to be finished, the patient usually opens his or her eyes and slowly returns to the immediate consciousness of being in my office, and I semi-shift out of facilitator role. "Semi-shift" because I want to come alongside the recipient as a witness and possible contributor to the work of the Spirit, rather than returning to a counselor role. I am still listening to the Holy Spirit on the inside, trying to discern whether He wants me to add in any words of knowledge, Scripture, impressions, or images that might have come to me during the session.

What takes place in the *direct encounter* of a person with the Lord is the most effective interaction. I do not want to interfere with His work for the day so I remain in an assisting role. The patient is usually absorbing and assimilating what has just happened. It is not an appropriate time to have an analyzing, dissecting debrief. I ask how the person is feeling and carefully add into the conversation any contributions I feel led to share.

I stay aware of the Lord's Presence and move towards a prayer of thanksgiving. Sometimes spontaneous prayer is initiated by the patient—usually words of gratitude and relief. Sometimes I pray and offer for the recipient to join in.

Throughout the Inner Healing session, I avoid having recipients say repeat-after-me prayers, whether confessing, thanksgiving, releasing, or receiving. I encourage them to take a few moments and then speak from the heart.

I will now make the essential elements of Inner Healing ministry more vivid by presenting a session with a patient. This session took place about two years ago. I hope that the steps I have just outlined will come alive for you as we go inside Annie's encounter with the Lord.

Chapter 17

A Lost Sheep Is Found: an Inner Healing Session with Annie

Annie returned for a third Inner Healing session. She reported that long-standing walls of self-protection were greatly diminished. She felt more relaxed and less guarded, evidenced by her willingness to share her heart more openly with her husband—something that had been difficult to do. She said that she noticed a big difference.

Annie had been ready for Inner Healing when she first came in for therapy. There had been abuse in her childhood and she knew that because of it she was blocking and deflecting God's love and the love of her husband. In the past, Annie had received counseling and prayer but walls still remained, leaving her weary and desperate. Inner Healing for the abuse had gone well in our previous times together and the walls were coming down, but she knew there were unresolved issues. Although she did not know where they were coming from, she still had unsettled feelings in various social interactions. She had returned on this day to let the Lord show her the origin of these feelings.

We began with prayer, invoking Matthew 18:20: "For where two or three are gathered together in My name, I am there in the midst of them." We first took some time to soak in this acknowledgment, and then I prayed aloud that the Holy Spirit would help Annie to perceive His Presence, in whatever way He chose. I further invited Him to do whatever ministry He intended for today. A minute passed and Annie reported that she was experiencing God's Presence with her. We waited expectantly for a starting place. Previously Annie had indicated that she was willing for the Lord to search her heart.

She closed her eyes during the opening prayer and, after a few moments of waiting on the Lord, she said that she felt a lack of peace when around her children. Pictures of interactions with her children had come to the forefront of her mind, accompanied by vague, unsettling feelings. "I'm just not at peace. Something's wrong there," she noted.

I prayed for the Holy Spirit's guidance. After a few moments, a memory of Annie at age ten came to her mind. Her father had abandoned the family when Annie was six years old, after which her mother had several boyfriends. One of the men, Ken, had been with her mother for two years and Annie had become attached to him. He had been tender and affectionate with her. The memory was a scene in which Annie vividly remembered standing in the driveway, watching Ken storm out of the house and drive away, never to return. I encouraged her to place herself into the memory and experience it as she had felt it at the time. She began to feel the pain as she watched Ken leave, just as her father had done four years earlier.

The memory-picture quickly shifted to a few months after this driveway event. Annie saw Ken at her friend's house. He had married her friend's mother. Ken was cold and distant, almost mean towards Annie. All the pain of rejection from her father, and now Ken, enveloped and almost overwhelmed her. I asked Annie if she could still experience the Presence of the Lord with her. She nodded in acknowledgment. He was there with her. Without any prompting, she continued: "Jesus has His arm around me in the memory. He is protecting me and comforting me. He's letting me know it's okay. He has a better plan for me."

With this disclosure from the Lord, Annie proceeded to release all the pain and rejection from the memory to the Lord. As she did, I quoted Isaiah 53, showing that since Jesus had carried our pain and sorrow, she could indeed release all of this pain onto Him. The release came in great sobs that had been packed away for many years. She then let the Comforter pour in His balm of peace and love onto her.

In the calm, I asked if she had ever forgiven Ken and her father. Years ago she had forgiven her father, and it was not difficult for her to forgive Ken and release him to the Lord. However, as she did so, a memory-picture of her mother flashed before her, and she realized that she had held her mother responsible. Ken's rejection came because her mother ruined the relationship with him. That is the belief she had internalized and held for many years.

Now several scenes with her mother arose in her mind. Her mother had been a very emotionally needy woman and Annie had felt like she was "her little slave." Fresh pain came, along with anger and resentment, as she felt the painful consequences of having a self-centered mother. "It was all about her, all the time," she cried out. "There's just so much pain because of her. I felt so used." At the Spirit's prompting, I knew she had to explore and eventually forgive her mother for all we had uncovered.

After a few minutes of listening to her enumerate her mother's offenses, I asked Annie if she was willing to start by forgiving her mother for the pain from the incident with Ken. She paused a moment, then said she was willing. From there I coached her to observe that if the Holy Spirit showed her other incidents with her mother, she could forgive her for them as they came up.

For the next few minutes, Annie spoke audibly to the Lord, releasing her mom for the Ken incident and several other events that involved her mother. She openly confessed harboring the sins of anger and resentment, and then released her mom and the accompanying negative emotions to the Lord. Following that, she received His forgiveness and cleansing, making 1 John 1:9 a living Word in that moment: "If we confess our sins, He is faithful and just to forgive us our sins and to cleanse us from all unrighteousness."

I asked how she was feeling. She said she felt better about her mom, but there was numbness on the inside of her. She was perplexed about this. She began to sort out memories that came to mind: She had five brothers...as a child she had to be tough...her mother was tough. I asked for the Holy Spirit's guidance and made sure Annie was willing to explore whatever was going on. She was willing. I again prayed, asking the Holy Spirit to show her the truth of why she had numbed out.

Within moments, her face contorted in anguish. "I had to be invisible!" she exclaimed. She reported that she was seeing herself as a seven-year-old girl standing in her family living-room, looking lost and forlorn. The sense came to her that she had never felt accepted as a person in her own right, but rather thought of herself as someone who existed solely to serve and please her mother. An internalized belief then came forward in the memory and she said, without emotion: "I am not worth anything." The pain of feeling worthless had been overwhelming for her as a little girl. She realized that a coping mechanism of numbing the pain had kicked in and had remained in effect these many years.

Annie acknowledged that the Lord was still present with her in that memory, though the little girl stayed in a semi-shadowed place, unsure of what was in store for her. "Is the girl willing to listen to what the Lord might want to say to her?" I asked.

"Yes."

I prayed, "Lord Jesus, is it true that this girl is worth nothing? What is Your truth for her?"

After a few moments Annie reported, "Jesus said that what happened in my life as a little girl is not what He intended. He allowed it but He didn't intend that for her. He wants something else for her."

Now a chuckle from Annie: "Psalm 27:10 just came into my mind and I know it is for me:

'When my father and my mother forsake me, then the Lord will take care of me,' reads the verse."

"Can little Annie receive that truth?" I asked.

"She's not sure that it is meant for her," Annie replied.

I prayed again, "Lord Jesus, is that Scripture meant for little Annie?"

Then a remarkable thing happened. Without any suggestion or human intervention, an image of the Good Shepherd came into Annie's mind and into mine as well. In a flash it was clarified that little Annie was a lost sheep. Annie recounted aloud the story of Jesus going after and picking up the lost sheep when He found it. Now smiling and weeping replaced the anguish on Annie's face. "He has gathered her in His arms. She is receiving His embrace but is doubtful about whether it will last. I think she believes He will go away like all the rest."

The Holy Spirit suddenly prompted me to suggest reconciliation between Annie, little Annie, and the Lord. I recalled Jesus' prayer to His Father, "...that they may be one as We are one" (John 17:11). I let the verse remain in my mind, unspoken, and asked, "What do you want to tell the girl about whether she can trust Jesus?"

Annie let her adult faith open up as she preached a short version of the Gospel to little Annie, ending with the fact that Jesus would never leave her nor forsake her. He would always be there for her. She was passing on the truth that she had believed for years to a part of her soul that needed to hear the Good News. Annie had acted on Jesus' words, "Go and tell my brethren" (Matthew 28:10). I call it soul-evangelism.

Little Annie now received the truth of being a lost sheep who had been found, *and* the truth that Jesus would never leave her. Healing Love began to flow in. The little one relaxed in the arms of Jesus and received His Love. She was safe, she was home.

I completed the session by facilitating a brief action of Annie taking the little girl into her heart. She assured the little one that she too would never leave her.

Annie opened her eyes. There was a peace in her eyes I had not seen before. "I feel much better," she said, with relief in her voice. She went on to say, "Oh, now I see what has been going on with my kids. Their needs have been overwhelming me. I have been trying to give them everything they want, compensating for what I didn't get from my mother." She admitted that she had been feeling anger and irritation at her kids but now knew where that was coming from—her own lost child who did not have her basic emotional needs met. "I think things will be different from now on," she concluded.[8]

We ended in prayer, thanking the Lord for His Presence, His guidance, and His healing. Annie's concluding prayer indicated that she had received and was beginning to internalize a new belief that she was a *person of value*, and that she had confidence God had equipped her to be a good mother to her children.

This session with Annie illustrates three main components of Inner Healing ministry:

1. Healing is making whole. It is restoring to wholeness what has been broken. Soul-integration happened in this session as Annie recognized and was united to the broken part of her that believed it had no worth and didn't belong. Also, this outcast-part needed to hear the message of acceptance in the Gospel. Annie, a believer, received Love and Light into a place in her soul that had been split off into darkness.

---

[8] In a subsequent phone call and in a later session, Annie indicated that her healing had remained, and that the situation with her children had cleared up considerably.

2. God's personal Presence heals. Annie acknowledged the Lord's Presence and invited Him to search her heart. The Holy Spirit illumined in Annie that painful place, an inner crevasse in which an abandoned child-part had lived alone. When I prayed and asked Jesus if Psalm 27:10 (God taking care of an abandoned person) was meant also for this lost part of Annie's soul, the Lord responded by giving an image that He alone inhabits: The Good shepherd. He brought the truth of the Good Shepherd relating to a lost sheep. Healing Love flowed into Annie through this image.

3. Sin and wounds are intertwined. Her mother had no doubt been injured in her own childhood and became emotionally needy, to the extent that she had *drawn* life from Annie as a child rather than *nurturing* Annie. This injured Annie deeply, and the trauma left a murky quagmire of pain, fear, anger, and resentment. She released the pain and fear to the Lord, letting Him dispose of that burden. She also confessed the hidden sins of anger and resentment, receiving God's forgiveness and cleansing. The releases of both sin and of pain were restorative actions of Inner Healing. By the power of the Holy Spirit, Jesus manifested Himself as both Savior and Healer.

The following is Annie's testimonial, written more than two years after this session:

> Starting the process of inner healing was a bit daunting for me. I guess when things got overly dark in my life I was willing to step out in courage. Jesus says, "Come to me...I am gentle and humble in heart, and you will find rest for your souls" (Matthew 11:28-29). That is the Jesus I found as I entered the inner healing experience. As I was prayerfully drawn back to painful childhood experiences, it was a great relief to regain those moments while releasing the associated hurt and bitter feelings. As I experienced the presence of Jesus with me in the pain, knowing he removes the shame and doesn't add to it, I was able to start a new journey in my life toward facing truth and not living with suppressed pain. The most dramatic change has been in my relationship with my Mom. Everything about

her used to anger me, but now I can love her and enjoy her as she is. It is amazing how forgiveness changes everything! -Annie

Chapter 18

The Inner Child of Our past

Similar to *inner healing*, the term *inner child* has been adopted by New Age spiritualities and psychotherapies. In several systems, it goes far beyond a way to express childhood experiences in memories. The term is tied into the all-is-One spirituality in which the inner child becomes "the Divine Child" or the "True Self." Let me simply state that these terms and their meanings are *not* what I intend in using the term inner child. But inner child, meaning *the inner child of our past*, is a meaningful image in emotional healing and should be retained.

Annie had accepted the Lord years before she came to Inner Healing sessions. She had been found by Him and knew Him as the Good Shepherd, along with other names, but there was a part of her soul that was living in darkness. She thought she had given her whole heart to the Lord but a part of her heart had remained in the shadows, living in solitude through a belief of *being unworthy*. The Lord reconciled a lost part of Annie's soul to Himself. He enfolded this part of Annie into His loving arms.

There is a principle stated in 1 Corinthians 13:11: "When I was a child, I spoke as a child, I understood as a child, I thought as a child; but when I became a man, I put away childish things." The Greek word for childish is *nepios*, which refers to childhood in an unhealthy way. It means being stuck in childhood when developmentally one should have grown beyond it. The word for "put away," *katergeo*, means to render powerless, or to get free from that which has been keeping one bound up (Seamands, 1985, p.286).

The unfortunate interpretation given to this passage (which I have heard more than once from pulpits) is a form of *spiritual repression*. The sermon goes something like this: "We need to stop ruminating about the past. Just focus on the Lord and let the Holy Spirit take you forward. Stop whimpering about what happened in the past. It's over, done with. Move on. God is in the present and in your future, not in your past." This is the type of simplistic teaching that induces needless guilt in people.

The context of the passage in 1 Corinthians 13 is the great chapter on love that begins, "Though I speak with the tongues of men and of angels, but have not love...." The chapter is about the characteristics and behavior of *agape* love which requires emotional and spiritual maturity. A usual reason one is *childish* instead of mature is because some experience in the past has remained unresolved. The incident was never fully processed and stays bound up in the soul, like a gear that gets stuck and can't move forward.

Here is a quick look at how this works. A person is traumatized, abused, or experiences a painful incident when a child. The pain and fear exceed the child's capacity to hold and process the volume of emotion. The emotional control center becomes overloaded and shuts down, similar to when we have too much physical pain—we shut down and lose consciousness. The whole incident can become repressed or shunted to a more remote, hidden part of the person's memory. However, it is not true in this case to say "out of sight, out of mind." It all gets recorded—the feelings, thoughts, beliefs, smells, sights, sounds—everything we experience is somewhere in our memories.

In trauma, when an emotional overload occurs, it is like pushing a pause-button on a TV remote control. The memory freezes in time in an unresolved state. The pain and fear are still there, clogging up the soul *in the present*, trying to push into consciousness to be processed. This unresolved emotional content is what sometimes makes adults act childishly.

To tell someone who is emotionally stuck in this way to just "get over it" is to keep him in a state of denial and repression. This is similar to a father looking over his newspaper to see what all the screaming and crying is about...and, when he sees his six-year-old son standing there with a badly gashed leg from falling off his bicycle, tells his son not to think about it. "Just get over it, you will be fine. What has happened has happened. It's in the past." The child needs attention not exhortation.

The word *katergeo* (1 Corinthians 13:11) does not mean *shove it aside* or put it behind you in an unresolved state. It means *to deal with the situation* so it can be put to rest...to resolve the issue so it no longer has the power to bind or hamper.

Inner child is an imaginative picture, conveying, mediating, and bringing something invisible into a visible form. I retain the term because I have found that there is an inner child of the past in our souls. And this image is especially real and full of feelings if incidents have happened that were not processed, resolved, or assimilated at the time they occurred.

It is not literal in a physical sense—there isn't a little kid running around on the inside of us. We develop adult bodies and our minds grow as we grow in knowledge; but we can have experiences in which feelings become bound-up inside, congealing around certain life-events. The feelings don't grow apace with the body and mind but are stuck in an unresolved memory. An entire memory can freeze in time, sealed as it originally happened, containing the emotional content like an invisible holding tank.

When a traumatic or painful memory finally emerges from the hidden part of the mind and comes into consciousness, it comes not as a disjointed tangle of thoughts and feelings (unless severely repressed because severely traumatic). The unresolved, unprocessed content appears in a personal way. Very often *the memory of the child who experienced the event is preserved*. Sometimes when the unresolved pain pushes forward with an urgency to express, the adult can feel like his whole self is absorbed into the child in the memory. He relives it as though it was happening now, and he identifies with this child-part as *himself* rather than a *part* of himself. It is important to know what is really going on.

Years ago, a man came to me as a patient. I was a Christian counselor, not yet trained in Inner Healing. Steve was a Christian man trying to live a Christian life but he had been depressed for many years and was currently taking medication.

He began telling his life-story. At age twelve his mother died. His father, a stern man, lined up all his children before going to the funeral and instructed them that there were to be no tears. Their mother was in a better place, he said, and they should be happy for her. With that they went to the funeral. There were no tears from any of them.

Steve resumed telling the story of how his life went on after that event. I interrupted and asked if he had ever grieved the death of his mother. He said he had felt sadness but went on with his life. "I got over it," he said. The heaviness of depression was in his voice. I asked if he remembered being at the funeral and would he be willing to go to that memory. A few moments passed. He said that he remembered standing next to his mother's coffin, peering inside to see her. "What are you feeling as you stand there?" I asked.

"I don't feel anything." He paused, and then added, "I wasn't allowed to feel anything."

"Steve, your father is gone and you are a man now. You can give yourself permission to feel and express it now, if you want to."

A few moments passed. His face began to change as pain welled up in it (Later he told me that he inwardly revoked the no-feeling rule imposed by his father and gave himself permission to feel.). He began to cry, at first in sputters and spurts. Then great sobs, like waves, rolled through his body. Tears flowed freely...for 30 minutes. These were not the tears of a 52 year-old man reflecting on his mother's death and crying about it. These were the tears of the twelve-year-old in Steve, the inner child of his past who had experienced that event.

The experience was still there, stuck, unresolved, unexpressed, repressed...as though an invisible pause-button on an inner remote control had been depressed these many years. The button was released when adult Steve gave the twelve-year-old permission to tell the truth of how he really felt.

In subsequent sessions, Steve's depression began to lift as he continued giving himself permission to feel. Gradually he was able to be weaned off his anti-depressant medication. He unlocked one memory after the other, and life began to flow through his body as he allowed his soul to feel and express his emotions. It had never occurred to him to declare his father's no-feeling rule null and void, but when he did so it had the effect of changing him towards becoming the man he was intended to be.

I do not know if Steve had heard sermons about getting his focus off the past and putting the past behind him, but that is what he had tried to do for years. However, that past memory had a lot of *present* power in it—the energy of pain, grief, and sadness, still intact after many years.

He had put the past behind himself in an *unhealthy* way. Now he "put it away" in a *healthy* way. The power of pent-up grief was drained out of his soul. He had finally grieved the death of his mother. New freedom emerged through the emotional release and he could set the event to rest, i.e., leave it in the past without pain and sorrow trying to push through—as they had been trying to do for 40 years. He could *katergeo* it, as described in 1 Corinthians 13:11.

Steve's story demonstrates that injuries and beliefs don't go away or lose their power through the passage of time or because we stop thinking about them. The way to allow something to be at rest in the past is to resolve it.

Chapter 19

Recipients of Inner Healing Tell Their Stories

The following statements are verbatim quotes from recipients of Inner Healing. I asked recipients and patients to respond to these questions: Was your life changed in any way as a result of your Inner Healing sessions? Did any healing take place? If there were changes or healing, have they lasted? From your experience, would you recommend this approach to others? The testimonies:

When I was twelve years old, a traumatic incident that I experienced gave Satan an opportunity to plant a lie in my soul so deep that it governed my thinking, emotions, and will for the next forty years. The lie gave me a pervasive sense of insecurity which caused me to doubt that God was really in control and that He would take care of me. I mostly lived a fearful life for those forty years, culminating in an emotional breakdown.

During an inner healing session in Washington D.C. at the turn of the century, an inner healing minister brought me back to that event and helped me replace Satan's lie with God's truth, and the stronghold that had gripped me for forty years was broken. I have proceeded on from that day with the realization that Jesus loves me and will always be with me – through all troubles and trials, as well as through all the good times. This reality is as certain as the air I breathe in to sustain my physical life.

❖ *PD*

I am a 46 year old woman and I experienced my first inner healing session about 6 years ago—it has totally changed my relationship with God. I always believed in God, accepted Jesus when I was young, and strayed away from my faith in my 20's and early thirties. I was emotionally unhealthy and in a great deal of pain. God kept leaving me breadcrumbs and wooing me back... I wanted a relationship with him, but not the kind from my childhood that was so fear-based and performance driven.

Now, I am actually grateful for the pain (most days) because it drove me to inner healing out of desperation. I was told that my beliefs were driving the emotions and that God could help change the beliefs. What I discovered was absolutely amazing.... God met me vividly in my imagination. He met me in the painful places and showed me who he was, and who I am. I experienced him and over time developed a trusting relationship.

I KNOW now that God meets me in the deepest, most painful places. He was kind and generous and never, ever pushy. My boundaries were mine and respected (unlike how it felt in childhood), and I really do trust him now, in ways I never experienced before.

Now, when I am anxious or in pain, I know he is there, waiting for me. And I don't need to fear him. I sometimes fear my own thoughts, but I know he is a safe place. This makes it easier to resist behaviors that, out of desperation, I clung to for security. I have a long way to go, but I have an experience-base now to draw from. I am so very grateful for that – it's priceless!

❖ *LC*

My name is K. I am 60 years old. I have been married for 28 years and have been a believer for about 30 years. Even though I was a believer I was addicted to pornography. It was my drug of choice. I started working with Dr. Day because it, my drug addiction, was affecting my relationship with God my marriage and family. It got to a point where I had to make a choice between God and my marriage, or pornography and lose it all.

With Dr. Day's facilitation and the leading of the Holy Spirit, we delved into events in my past which had caused me to withdraw from life and had opened the door to the fantasy life pornography provides. With the help of the Holy Spirit, God showed me His view of these events and how He always was there loving me, not judging me. He saw me as a winner. Once I was able to accept His interpretation of these events and incorporate them into my life I have been able to rededicate and energize my relationships with God, my marriage, my children and grandchildren. I am happy to report that the addiction to pornography is gone.

 K

Inner healing has changed my life in a huge way. I cannot say enough good things or praise the Lord enough for all that He has done through the work of the Holy Spirit during inner healing sessions.

I am a 45 year old wife and mom, and like most people, I've been deeply wounded by others who have sinned against me and by my own sinful actions. I was a victim of sexual abuse as a child, struggled with sexual sin as a teen/young adult, and was devastated by a broken engagement while in college. But the biggest blow came when I was 35 and my husband of over 10 years told me he was struggling with habitual sexual sin. I was undone; more hurt, angry, distraught, confused and depressed than ever before. I've known Christ as Savior since I was a young girl and my Heavenly Father has carried me through every trial in life, so I knew the Lord was my only hope. My husband and I sought Biblical counseling.

We found a husband/wife team; for me it was helpful, for my husband it was torture. We cried, we talked and we prayed together. By God's mercy and grace we began to put our marriage back together little by little. Over the years that followed, I did numerous Bible studies, saw two other Christian counselors for several months at a time and read/devoured every Christian counseling book on marriage and that I could find. But the deep pain often returned, resurfacing in my heart and mind whenever I encountered a memory trigger and when I least expected it. It was haunting.

Then the Lord led us to return to counseling and Bill helped me to look at my deepest wounds and lay them at the Savior's feet. The Lord used the inner healing sessions to speak to me in a very personal and powerful way. I was utterly amazed after the first session. The rapid progress I had made in just one session was amazing. I myself am a counselor (for abused children) and I had never experienced such healing in such a short period of time.

My husband's inner healing sessions were just as astounding. The Lord used just a few sessions to reveal and heal many wounds from child abuse in his life. The spiritual healing and wholeness that are now a part of our everyday lives is amazing, priceless, and life transforming. We truly know what it means to be free—free from pain, free from anger and bitterness, free from emptiness and loneliness, but most of all free from the chains of habitual sin. We are truly new creatures in Christ, free to let God's love flow through us—to accept His love for us and then let it flow out to each other and to those around us. Everything is NOT perfect, we continue to struggle with sinful hearts and the sin in our world. But we know our Father and healer so much better; we know where to turn when life is hard and how to meet Him in the deep places.

❖   *(anonymity requested)*

Inner healing ministry has taken me spiritually where Bible intake and traditional counseling simply could not. As a pastor, I wholeheartedly affirm the dire need for solid Bible teaching and other conventional spiritual disciplines, but I now see inner healing as an incredibly valuable aspect of the sanctification journey. Through inner healing, I have come to truly know God as Father, to recognize the voice of my Shepherd, and to appreciate more dearly the ministry of the Holy Spirit.

While space does not allow me to enumerate the details of all I have received over the years, I will say that God has used it to set me free from controlling rage and crippling lies. After graduating seminary and serving vocationally as a pastor for several years, I cognitively knew that God loved me and that I was accepted by His grace, but I cannot say that this was my day by day reality. It was no problem for me to write papers and deliver messages on the extravagance of God's love available because of Jesus' sacrifice on the cross. However, the experiential reality of my life was anger, self-hatred, and exhausting religious performance.

Since my first inner healing session in May of 2002, I have both been the recipient in and facilitated many inner healing sessions, and, because of this, my walk with the Lord has been radically different. I have witnessed God speaking powerfully time and time again, setting me and others free from soul wounds and lies. Total healing will not take place until we are glorified and fully in the presence of Jesus, but inner healing has been a significant aspect of my movement into that wholeness. All glory and praise go to God alone, and I thank Him for the transformation I have received through inner healing ministry.

❖ *GMc*

During my life, I have participated in three different Christian Counseling programs. My first two experiences were conducted by trained Christian Counselors using conventional techniques. While these sessions were helpful, the process seemed to provide assistance by examining past behavior and encouraging future habits based on traditional Christian values. I found these Christian Counseling programs helpful, but the knowledge and lessons I took from these sessions were mostly intellectual and at a surface level.

The Inner Healing sessions with Dr. Bill Day were much different than the traditional Christian Counseling programs I had experienced in the past. The Inner Healing sessions not only involved an intellectual examination, it involved an emotional exchange as well. This was an incredibly powerful experience, and provided an inner peace I have not experienced in a long time. During the Inner Healing session, Dr. Day asked that we invite Christ into the room and talk with him as I would another person. Despite being a Christian my entire life, this was the first time I had experienced a truly personal relationship with the Lord.

The entire process functioned like a blood transfusion where contaminated emotions such as guilt and regret were exchanged for fresh, clean thoughts and feelings. This process provided an immediate positive impact in my life. In addition, the benefits I received through the Inner Healing process have remained with me through time.

I believe the Inner Healing techniques have been successful because my experience was not simply intellectual, but also deeply emotional. This process was a very personal and intimate experience that has made a lasting impact in my life.

❖ *GM*

My husband and I have been married for almost six years now. My husband began seeing Dr. Bill for inner healing sessions during our courtship, and shortly after we were married I began to consider going myself. Our first two years of marriage were difficult; we were desperate for the Lord to break through in our lives and in our marriage. At first I was a bit reluctant to go and make myself so vulnerable by opening up to someone I did not know, and quite frankly, to the Lord as well. I knew I could not hide! I had already been introduced to the concept of listening prayer and experienced a taste of it through several friends.

Finally, I began going to see Dr. Bill on my own. Each session was so powerful. It's never been about someone giving me advice about how to think about something differently or striving to believe a truth I already know. My inner healing sessions with Dr. Bill were him facilitating prayer and giving me the opportunity to have an encounter with the Lord. The freedom I've experienced has been lasting because it was an actual experience of hearing the voice of Jesus tell me the truth in place of a lie I had been believing for so long. There's something so powerful about that. I learned that even physical manifestations can be tied to root beliefs we have about something. On one occasion as soon as God exposed a false belief I had about something and revealed His truth to me, I immediately relaxed on the inside and was healed of a chronic digestive issue I had been struggling with.

I've experienced spiritual, mental, emotional, and physical freedom through inner healing. My husband and I never once had a joint session, but as we've received our own healing it was amazing how our marriage began to improve significantly. That has really spoken volumes to me that it's about each of us letting the Lord come into those broken places and making us whole that strengthens our relationship, not airing our grievances and expecting the other person to change.

We are now on the mission field full time in Africa and are able to continue the process of listening prayer here as the Lord brings to light areas where we still need His love and truth to come in and transform us. The Lord is so eager and faithful to meet us in those places when we open ourselves to an encounter with Him. It can be scary at times, but it's so worth it! He wants to set us free.

 GC

The many testimonies that poured in from recipients provide confirming evidence of the Lord's intention to heal troubled hearts. I am grateful to those who took time to speak out. My apologies for leaving out some testimonies; it was a matter of space, not quality, that was the determining factor. Every testimony was inspiring.

Chapter 20

Inner Healing and Christian Counseling

Although this chapter is intended for all readers, I am directly addressing my colleagues here. Sometimes we are called *caregivers*. This includes Christian counselors, psychologists, psychotherapists, psychiatrists, pastors, and lay ministers. This chapter is about God being the primary Caregiver: "...casting all your anxiety on Him, because He cares for you" (1 Peter 5:7 NASB).

The Power to Heal

Most in the field of Christian counseling and ministry accept the basic premise that deception and lies lead to the trouble in human lives and that God's truth will set us free. But do we take Jesus literally when He says "I am...the truth" in John 14:6? An approach that I practiced for years is expressed in the principle: *truth = true information*. This approach relies on varieties of cognitive therapies and behavioral therapies (a focus on problem-solving strategies to change unwanted behavior). Such methods have value but sometimes leave out the inner heart—places in our souls that are not immediately accessible in daily, function-focused consciousness.

While here on earth, Jesus was aware that deep within us are hidden beliefs, and if left in the dark such beliefs will do great damage. As the living Word, He had Proverbs 23:7 within Himself: As a person "thinks in his *heart* so is he" (emphasis mine). In stories, parables, and powerful images, Jesus exposed darkened regions of the heart with the blazing light of His truth.

Two examples come to mind. In the incident with the rich young man, He uncovered the hidden character of the man's earthly attachment with a few words about selling his riches... "and come follow me" (Matthew 19:21). Jesus was lovingly after the man's heart. The invitation was for the man to release his attachment and receive what would come from following Jesus. In a second recorded incident, Jesus told the woman caught in adultery to "go and sin no more" (John 8:11), but only after He changed out her sin with His forgiveness and dissolved her shame with the love that I'm sure streamed from His eyes down into her heart.

Traditional counseling can be much like handing a compass to a man who has little or no direction in life—and sometimes this is appropriate and helpful. Counseling sessions can be replete with biblical principles, advice, strategies...as well as guidelines from various psychological systems that seem compatible with biblical principles. Some positive changes often happen with these approaches. For example, through the questions and knowledge of a counselor, a patient can take the lid off repressed or confused emotions and begin to see into the tangles of his or her soul for perhaps the first time. This is an important process of self-discovery.

But sometimes in the counseling process, a person comes upon darkened areas of the soul that have been malformed by distorted perceptions about God, self, and relationships with others. These perceptions can be formed in childhood when minds are so impressionable, and skewed perceptions may also be formed by traumatic experiences in adulthood.

These areas are the unsurrendered places in our souls that defiantly or fearfully oppose any light that tries to enter. These are the shadowy places in which habituated self-devised ways of coping and surviving dwell. Also, in these areas entrenched beliefs reside, such as: *no one will take care of me so I have to take care of myself.*

With stubborn pseudo-independence these beliefs oppose thoughts of God's love and provision even when such positive thoughts flash like neon signs from our mind's storehouse of words and concepts. And sometimes the living Word of God Himself is the power needed to overcome such opposition.

The counselor hopes for the right words to say, the right Scriptures to assign, and the right insights to quash and crowd out the lies that have emerged from a patient's childhood or adult years. Lies such as, *It was my fault that my father molested me*, or, *I am worthless and unlovable.* But sometimes our words: "It wasn't your fault" or "God loves you" do not have the power to penetrate the dark, hard membrane of long-held beliefs.

Please hear me: I believe that a counselor's words of compassion, insight, and truth can help and have a beneficial effect...but sometimes in the dark recesses of a patient's soul only the Presence of Love Himself can vanquish fear and darkness.

My initial suggestion to my Christian counseling brothers and sisters is to consider that the truth that sets us free is the person of Jesus. Advice, counsel, and written words of truth may be helpful; but in an encounter with the paralyzing darkness of lies and deception, I ask you to consider the course of action given in the aforementioned Mark 2:4 passage: to lower the paralytic into the Presence of Jesus.

When *He* says to the person who is still anguishing in guilt as she remembers her sexual abuse: "It was not your fault", His words can blast away the dark guilt, if a person is willing to receive and internalize His words as truth. And when a person is groveling in the dark despair of feeling worthless and unlovable—and hears the gentle yet authoritative voice of Jesus say "I love you and will always be with you,"—the penetrating light of His truth can shatter and disperse this despair.

For full healing, layers of lies may need to be uncovered over time but, in an initial flash, a person can go from the depths of despair to a place of hope that feels every bit like release from prison—and it lasts. I have been released from such imprisonment and have witnessed the release of many captives.

The Healing Process

Then there is the matter of the nature of the healing process. As Christian practitioners and ministers, what are we trying to accomplish? How do we know when a client, recipient, or patient is really being healed? What role do we have in the healing process?

When I first became a Christian counselor, I saw little difference between how my Christian colleagues practiced cognitive therapy and how my former secular colleagues practiced, except Christians used biblical thoughts. In both cases the therapists stayed in the *driver's seat,* using the mind to analyze, understand, give advice, and create problem-solving strategies. The goals were also similar: to reduce stress, enhance a sense of wellbeing, improve relationships, and develop personal growth as an individual.

Here is the issue: If we are to practice or minister in a different way than the world—because we are counselors or ministers in the Kingdom of God—then we are *theocounselors, theopsychologists,* and *theotherapists.* We are not our own. We have turned our lives over to God and His purposes. In conducting therapy sessions, we are to start with Him and His concerns, not ours.

It is clear from the beginning that God created humans in His likeness. But streaming through us—as a river with strong currents—are tendencies towards evil that we inherit from ancestors, going back to Adam. The fallen state of mankind is not like a fall from a bicycle resulting in knee gashes. Our human condition is immersed in darkness so thick that only God's power can penetrate it. Jesus came to pull us out of this darkness. Tinkering with the human condition by a change here, an adjustment there—or strategies for coping and adapting—doesn't even scratch the surface of the actual human condition. It is not *change* that is warranted, it is *exchange.*

The entire story of the world can be told in the core mystery of the Gospel of Jesus Christ, i.e., the Reconciliation of 2 Corinthians 5:18-20. God's intentions for us are revealed there: to return to a relationship of being a friend of His. Isn't that what we believe as Christian therapists: that down deep everyone is looking for this Friend, and that He planted this desire within us...the God-shaped hole that can only be filled by God?

There is a relationship between healing, wholeness, and holiness in that the context for healing is a restoration of what has been broken... and what has been broken is our connection with God as children in His family. How would any of us parents feel if our children believed lies about us: that we don't love them, that we think they will never amount to anything, or that we have written them off because they have messed up so often? We would want to look our children in the eyes and blast away such lies with the truth of our love. I believe that this is often what God wants to do.

Sometimes Surgery is Necessary

Perhaps your vocation is to give clients a compass and help them find direction through sound biblical counseling. Perhaps there are many thoughts that need to be exchanged at the immediate-consciousness level as clients begin their journeys towards wholeness and holiness. There is a place for that kind of counseling, and I know it helps in the healing process. My hope is that you will know when to refer folks for surgical removal of deeply embedded, spiritually cancerous soul-growths that cannot be removed by traditional counseling.

I have a fairly steady stream of patients who have been in traditional, cognitive Christian counseling and have come away disappointed that they have received only temporary relief from their symptoms. Over time the same problems settled back in and continued to plague them. In some cases new beliefs developed, such as: *I just can't get it, there must be something wrong with me.*

Such is the risk of a Christian therapist staying in the mind, using it to figure out, to impart information (true though it may be), to give the mind a *directing* role. Directing is a burden that the mind is not designed to carry. The mind is part of the soul and is to be in a *servant* role. When the Holy Spirit comes to dwell within a person, the days of the mind as alpha dog are over. Further, the minds of both counselor and recipient have vast tracts of false beliefs, skewed interpretations, doubts about God, and other malformations. Even as partially sanctified, the mind is not fit to be director of operations.

My suggestion is for you to consider receiving healing and training in Spirit-led ministry. If you choose to remain totally within traditional counseling methodology, then please consider referring patients to an Inner Healing specialist at the appropriate time. We in Inner Healing aren't "specialists" in the sense of being experts; it's just that we are called into facilitating the exchanges that require God's direct, interactive intervention. Sometimes surgery is necessary.

If you are a Spirit-led Christian counselor, perhaps you are already allowing the Holy Spirit to guide you into the depths of troubled hearts.

I invite you to look into methods of Inner Healing; perhaps you will find resources there that can add to the effectiveness of your therapy.

The Role of Counseling Before and After Surgery

Before. There are times when I sit with patients and wear a counselor's hat. When I first begin with a recipient, there is an initial goal of building trust. I know that there is a protective part of the person, a part that is vigilantly checking me out: Is this guy safe? Does he know what he is doing? Is he likely to harm or help? What is his intention in wanting access to my painful parts?

In light of these unspoken yet probing questions, it is important to let Jesus' character of compassion reach out towards a patient's *protector*, welcoming that part into any plan or procedure. Also, compassion is communicated by eye-contact, tone of voice, and choice of words. Sometimes it is possible to look into a patient's eyes and see an abandoned child who is checking for any evidence of judgment from me.

As I listen to a patient's issues and life-story, I am silently praying, asking the Holy Spirit for discernment and guidance. As led, I give initial responses which may include descriptions of my therapeutic approach, and personal and professional background information. In building trust and a sense of safety, people want to have evidence of expertise in soul-navigation, and that the therapist also has a sack of rocks which he has had to learn how to carry.

I clearly indicate to them that the call on my life is to be an instrumental part of the healing that God intends for them, but that I am coming alongside them as a fellow pilgrim, walking the same path of seeking truth. Then I identify my upcoming role to be that of a facilitator and an assistant to the "Counselor" (Isaiah 9:6), who is Jesus and His Holy Spirit.

I also discuss my role as that of a coach who will work to bring into the open the Lord's invitations. As part of this latter discussion I make sure to clarify the significant and essential role that their choices have. I let them know that nothing will happen apart from them willingly choosing either to change or to allow changes.

Throughout this first session, or sessions, it is important to sense the degree of readiness and need for surgery that the patient may or may not have. I don't push for Inner Healing. Good barometers for determining readiness are: a high level of desperation and weariness, a realization of personal powerlessness, and willingness to jump in fully to let the Lord lead.

Sometimes a person is immediately ready; sometimes counseling sessions are needed to build trust and safety, or to loosen up any resistance or defenses that may strongly present themselves. When a patient is prepped for soul-surgery, usually it is clear both to me and to the person. Then we go forward, in the power and presence of the Healer, the Lover of our souls.

After. As indicated in Chapter 16, sharing my thoughts and impressions can have a role in helping a patient to assimilate the experience. Additionally, a separate follow-up session(s) is often necessary to strengthen and deepen the healing. The complexity of hurtful memories involves not only the intense pain held inside for many years but also the dysfunctional and sometimes sinful ways one has chosen to cope with situations and people.

The survivor-self in us has insinuated itself into our personality in layers of coping patterns. Like the layers of an onion, they are often brought into the open one at a time. Understanding, insight, mentoring, and meditating on the Word are all helpful ways to loosen and clarify these onion-layers, until the next one is ready to be surrendered into the exchange-process. Therapist and patient listen to the under-melody playing through their spirits during their conversations in these aftermath counseling sessions, waiting to sense together the Master's prompting that the time is at hand for more.

One day Jesus entered a synagogue. A man was there who had a withered hand. Jesus walked over to him and in effect said, "Your time has come, stretch out your hand if you want it healed." The man stretched it out to the Lord and his hand was "restored as whole" (Matthew 12:13). My patients and I listen together for such moments when Jesus will indicate the withered part whose time has come.

When that time arrives, I once again become the Master's assistant, asking the Holy Spirit to clarify which disfigured part of one's soul Jesus is standing in front of, beckoning the person to stretch it out to Him. Just as the man with the withered hand *chose in faith* to stretch out his hand to the Lord, so too does a recipient of Inner Healing choose to stretch out his or her withered part...to be restored and made whole. When the patient is ready the Master will be there. His heart is to forgive, to heal, to restore, to make whole, to make holy.

Chapter 21

The Perennial Problem of Self-Worth

Many books have been written on the subject of self-esteem, self-worth, self-love, and self-image. Beliefs of a diminished valuation of oneself feature in many maladies: anxiety, depression, addictions, eating disorders, and more. When these beliefs are extreme, e.g., *I am an outcast who is unlovable,* the process of healing can be difficult. If I believe *I am a loser*, this lie can be a strong mind-shield which deflects any thought of healing and success in life.

The question of worth has mostly been understood through the concept of a scale. This is a view of humans as containers who have measurable amounts of a substance called worth. *Worthless* (empty) is at one end of the scale, and *of intrinsic and eternal valu*e (full) is at the other end. I have found this to be a spiritually inaccurate way to look at the issue, and I offer an alternative view.

My Story of Self-worth

At age 42, when I encountered my heavenly Father for the first time, my mind was cluttered with conflicting notions about myself and God. From my Catholic upbringing I had internalized a view of myself as way down on the self-worth spectrum. Then, as a New Ager, I considered myself to be a "10" on the scale because of the belief of my supposed divinity and goodness. It took several years for God to untangle the snarl of my perceptions. As I released these conflicting views and exchanged them for truths spoken directly into my heart by the living Word of God, a new awareness dawned quietly in my soul: *Worth is a relational reality, not a measurable substance.*

The Presence of a loving Father seeped into my life. The offer of Jesus to "Abide in Me" became the way in which God conferred worth on me by loving me and lighting up the reality that I am His child. But I could only have that sense of worth by being in relationship with Him. I was the son in Jesus' prodigal son story, the son who returned to his father and lived out his days as a son in relation to his father.

I was indeed a *wretch,* which simply means a person who is in deep distress. I had filled the God-shaped hole in me with everything but God and had remained a wretch like the prodigal son in the pigsty.

It took many years but I finally discovered that God created a place for Himself in me, that it is a design-feature of my human nature and that of the patients whose journeys I witnessed. It's a *relational hole* that is filled by the dynamic of a relationship, not a *quantitative hole* that needs a substance to fill it. And when I received the reality of Him loving me, as a Father loving His son, He grafted me back into Himself and a sense of worth was conferred upon me in the context of relationship.

From the relational sense of worth that I now experience in living out my days as a son of my Father who is King of all, I believe that the self-worth scale presented at the beginning of this chapter is a false framework. To say that I am intrinsically good and have eternal worth and value in and of myself is not true. And it is also not true to say that I am a miserable wretch who is worthless.

Part of being created in God's image is an embedded relationship-design: that to be complete (and therefore whole and of worth) is to be relationally connected to Him. As framed in Augustine's prayer, "You have made us for Yourself, and our hearts are restless until they rest in You."

Self-worth According to Jesus

In Luke 18:9-14, Jesus tells a parable about a Pharisee and a tax collector. The Pharisee thought he had achieved high worth in himself by doing good deeds. In total contrast, the tax collector, acutely aware of his actual state of emptiness—simply called out to God to have mercy on him, an abject sinner. This is not another of Jesus' castigations of the Pharisees for hypocrisy. It is more a statement about a mistaken notion of self-worth and Jesus' presentation of the actual human condition for all mankind.

As stated above, it took years for truth to make its way into the layers of deception in my mind, but by God's mercy and love the veil fell from my eyes and I realized that *I was the tax collector*. Paradoxically, the journey to the Lord conferring worth upon me, in the context of relationship with Him, began by a heartfelt acknowledgment of my self-inflations of pride and arrogance, my defiance and disrespect of my Creator and Father...and the actual and utter spiritual emptiness of my soul. The real journey to true self-value began with declaring bankruptcy.

As I truthfully recognized my poverty and called out to God, as the tax collector that I was, He responded to my plea and my brokenness... and He grafted me into Himself. *Then* I had real value, as did the prodigal son when he returned to the embrace of his father and lived out his days in the family to which he belonged. The prodigal son and I both might technically have been of noble birth, but that fact alone would have been hollow had we stayed in our wretchedness. It is true that "God doesn't make junk." We humans have junked up His creation. I would certainly have continued doing so had I not returned to my Father, to live out my days as His son.

Living in the Kingdom/Family

There is a further dimension to plumb. In Luke 18:19 Jesus says that "only God is good." In Matthew 5:48 Jesus gives the exhortation: "Therefore you shall be perfect, just as your Father in heaven is perfect." If God alone is good, how can anyone be expected to be perfect?

To address this question, it is instructive to look at Luke 17:20-21. The Pharisees were questioning Jesus as to when the kingdom of God was coming. He replied by telling them that "the kingdom of God is in your midst." As He often did, Jesus shone a bright light into the deception-darkness of the blind Pharisees. Jesus, God-in-the-flesh, was Himself the kingdom of God standing right there in their midst. In His own Person He ushered in the rule and reign of God and invited humankind into this kingdom/family.

It is interesting that Jesus used family-imagery in speaking of being born again, or born from above (John 3:3). In the natural realm we are born into relationships, into a family where there is a sense of belonging, of being loved and loving in return. In 2 Corinthians 5:18-21, the imputation of Jesus' righteousness onto us is not solely an external covering-over of our sins like a garment that hides a permanently disease-ridden body. In God's family we are given the status of Christ's righteousness *while* we let God heal us and make us righteous, over time, by replacing our old nature with Jesus' nature. He is making us good with His Goodness; He is replacing our imperfections with the very perfect character of Jesus.

The only way I can be good or attain any measure of "being perfect as my heavenly Father is perfect" is to let the Holy Spirit continue to impart God's Life into me, not by exerting my human nature to try to be godly. I no longer try to salvage some remnant of respectability and self-worth from my old human nature. I can sense and recognize the Holy Spirit inserting Jesus' nature into my soul whenever I am willing to release old junk.

Through abiding in Jesus in His kingdom/family of God, He replaces *self* with *His Self* to create the Jesus-and-me composite indicated in Galatians 2:20: "It is no longer I who live, but Christ lives in me." *Releasing my old nature and taking on His nature is the God-ordained forge in which authentic self-worth is shaped.*

We have a popular question that has made its way into films, books, and onto wristbands: "What would Jesus do?" I believe Jesus would say in all situations, "Abide in Me and I in you so that you will gradually have My mind and heart...and then you will know what to do. And with My Life in you, you will be *able* to do it." Again, the process is the Lord *imparting*, not us *imitating*.

Lies and Truth about Self-worth in Inner Healing

Many of the lies that emerge in Inner Healing sessions come from the far side of the low end of the scale: *I'm worthless; I'm unlovable; I belong on the outside; I'm a loser.* Whether resulting from an absence of love or from outright injury and abuse, these beliefs deflect God's love, and often form negative beliefs about God: *God doesn't love me; God is not there and He doesn't care.* A person with such buried beliefs can feel extremely isolated and cut off from all resources.

When we pray in sessions and ask God for His truth, God does not respond and tell recipients that they are good or wonderful or just fine the way they are. Most responses are statements such as: "I love you; I will take care of you; I will never leave you; you are my beloved child." No responses ever suggest dropping more deeply into oneself, or "Get rid of the sin in your life and then we'll talk." The content and tone are personal, relational, and full of Lovingkindness.

It is curious that in the Bible sinners enjoyed Jesus' company. They felt comfortable with Him, not as though they were under an analytic gaze. It's not that Jesus was soft on sin—never was, never will be. It was because Jesus looked deep into their souls with love. In the presence of all others, the tax collectors and prostitutes felt like outcasts having no worth. Jesus held them in the embrace of enveloping Love, beckoning them to return home to family-life with their Father. In His presence they felt safe, loved, valued.

During Inner Healing sessions Jesus first says *Be Mine*, then focuses on *behavior*. In various ways He first imparts His love to a recipient, within which impartation He also gives the capacity to eliminate sin from one's life. A recipient has to receive His Truth, but it is His Truth in a person that makes her or his choices effective for consistently living a good life. This reception of Truth also brings healing.

Inner Healing is often necessary to get at embedded self-worth lies because the beliefs are often formed at an early age when a child is vulnerable and without a secure identity. Repeated phrases such as "you are stupid" become "I am stupid" on the inside of a child. Core-identity lies can become firmly fixed, impervious to human attempts in adult years that try to dislodge the beliefs.

However, amazingly, I have experienced God's power, like a laser beam, burning away such lies in me when focused directly on the beliefs—in the memory-places where the beliefs were inserted. And I have witnessed this same penetrating laser-Light in surgery-sessions with patients. God's searing Light dislodges and destroys lies that are released, and then the Light of His Truth shines in to take up lasting residence in the soul. When this happens, recipients experience new peace, perhaps for the first time, in those places in their souls.

From such experiences, and from seeing their effects afterwards, I have come to this conclusion: *True self-worth is the experience of being loved by our Father.* By receiving His Love, a person can be taken into a satisfying sense of being known and a sense of belonging—within which is the full measure of worth that the human heart desires.

> Do not fear, for I have redeemed you; I have called you by name; you are Mine!...since you are precious in My sight, since you are honored and I love you....Bring My sons from afar and My daughters from the ends of the earth, everyone who is called by My name, and whom I have created for My glory, whom I have formed, even whom I have made.
>
> (Isaiah 43:1-7 NASB)

Chapter 22

Special Issues

In this final chapter of PART III, I have selected four issues that have been significant in my healing and in the healing of patients through the years. Each section could have been developed into a separate chapter but I sense that what the Lord would have me express about Inner Healing is drawing to a close for now. It's a dense chapter; perhaps you could think of it as four mini-chapters.

• Dealing with the Demonic

The previous chapter on self-worth is a good segue into this first section because much of Satan's work involves mining the fields of distortions, false interpretations, and half-truths that are buried in human perceptions of self and of God. Usually one mines for gold or something precious; Satan mines for the "treasures" of pride and self-absorption...or the other end of the self-worth spectrum—shame and fear.

In previous chapters of this book, I have presented the step by step realization that God is the Designer of my life. My perception is that God has always been in loving pursuit, even when I fled Him down the highways and byways of life. In this God-story there is an antagonist, an arch-villain whose sole purpose on this earth is to move about in the spiritual realm, looking for ways to disrupt and destroy (1 Peter 5:8) the work of the Pursuer and Lover of my soul. We have to deal with this adversary who has many voices, and we all have gone astray (Isaiah 53:6) through his deceptions. It has been so since the beginning (Genesis 3).

Twenty years ago I participated in deliverance ministries in which Jesus' name was used in a loud voice, in attempts to drive out demons. We would have recipients renounce spirits of rejection, spirits of addiction, etc., and then the team of ministers would command the demons to leave in Jesus' name. Often a recipient would receive temporary relief of fear and other symptoms, but usually the troubling emotions and thoughts would return.

I remember bringing one of my patients to my pastor for a deliverance session. My patient had an addiction to viewing pornography and his marriage was falling apart. My pastor and I had the man renounce various spirits, and we waited to see the results. The use of pornography continued. As I went deeper into the man's addiction during subsequent therapy sessions, the Holy Spirit showed me the hidden belief that is present in many addictions: *I can't live without this drug*. We could have shouted the name of Jesus all day long, but a dark spiritual presence could hang around in the man's mind as long as he held onto that twisted belief. Part of his will was secretly latched onto that belief. It would take an act of his will to release the lie.

I liken the story of this man to the *exhortation method* of sermons in which the preacher tries to drive truth into the hearts of his listeners by the force of shouting, clear articulation, and repetition.

I stopped doing this type of deliverance ministry for the same reasons I left traditional cognitive Christian counseling to go into Inner Healing: neither practice was effective in dealing with embedded lie-based pain. When the lies are deep, the Holy Spirit is needed for finding them and His power is needed to accomplish the exchange of truth for lies. When the lie is gone and one is standing in the truth administered by the Holy Spirit, the recipient or facilitator can evict demonic intrusion. When the garbage is removed, it's not difficult to shoo away the flies. I have witnessed this process over and over as a powerful way to set captives free.

Jesus called Satan a "liar" (John 8:44), and he is called the "accuser" in Revelation 12:10. When someone believes a lie, he or she is standing on Satan's turf. It's a kind of spiritual enmeshment in which a person is susceptible to hearing a demon's voice echoing agreement with what the person believes. I listened to his slippery smooth voice for many years as I internalized the spiritual narcissism of New Age beliefs. In many ways he deceptively confirmed that I was on a "true path" to realizing my "divine nature." Later, he turned into an accuser who highlighted a residual heresy in my internalized belief system: *I had committed too many shameful, sinful acts to be fully forgiven.* As an accuser his voice changed to a raspy tone that was judgmental and critical.

My mind was held captive until I called out to the Lord for the truth that would set me free. He spoke His truth: "You are my son" into the place of the lie. I received this truth and was set free to be the man God called me to be.

Flies hang around garbage. Demons are like flies and lies are like garbage. I used to swat at flies in old-style deliverance ministry and now I focus on letting the Holy Spirit show me and recipients the garbage (lies) from which the stench (sin, pain, fear, shame, etc.) exudes. Once the garbage is removed and the smell goes away, the flies will leave. They have to. They have been defeated by the Person who holds all truth. Hebrews 2:14 and Colossians 2:13-15 tell us clearly that Jesus defeated the devil and rendered him powerless in the realm of His Truth. Satan's only power over us is when we are trafficking in lies.

The following is the way in which I now deal with the demonic in Inner Healing. In Chapter 16, I listed the steps of ministry that I follow. In Step 3d, when I discern that a recipient has fully released a lie that has been uncovered and is ready to receive Truth, I often insert a prayer of deliverance (an eviction notice) such as the one I prayed last week with a patient:

Lord, on the basis of Tom coming out of agreement with the belief that *I am not worth Your attention*, I stand with him on Your ground of Truth that You have shown him: that *You are with him and that You delight in him*. Because Tom has renounced and released the lie of unworthiness to you, we use the authority You gave us and, in the name of Jesus, we command any spirit or demon that was attached to this lie in his soul to get out and go to Jesus to be disposed of.

If recipients are mature in their faith and know the authority Jesus has given to His followers to dispel the demonic (Ephesians 1:20-21, Mark 16:17), they often join in this prayer.

There are complex situations in which demonic power features more prominently and there is a place for more elaborate deliverance ministry. In the AFTERSTORY, I direct you to resources I have found helpful so you can look into this matter further. The brief description in this section is the way in which Inner Healing is inherently a ministry of deliverance. Jesus came to destroy the works of the devil (1 John 3:8), which He did in the Reconciliation. One way this finished work of Jesus continues is when anyone allows the Holy Spirit to continue destroying lies with Truth through the exchanges that take place in Inner Healing.

- **The Power of Addiction**

The etymology of *addiction* is revealing. The word means *signed over to, devoted to, giving up to...a power outside of oneself*. It connotes a dynamic in which one places oneself into a servant/master relationship, agreeing to do the bidding of the power to which one gives oneself over.

I unwittingly initiated such a relationship when I began smoking cigarettes in college. I smoked for 25 years before I finally broke off the relationship for good. It took several quit-attempts but I finally succeeded after being humbled by many failed attempts.

As I was walking into a bookstore in Boston, my eyes focused on what I thought was a "NO SMOKING" sign on the back wall. A second glance clarified that the sign said "KNOW SMOKING." Within myself I sighed resignedly, "Alright, I want to know the truth about smoking."

The next morning when I awoke, two large-print words were front and center in my mind: MASTER and SLAVE. Immediately an understanding flowed around those words and I realized that if I retained any connection to nicotine—in body or mind—it would only be a matter of time before I would creep back into a relationship with the drug, a relationship in which the drug was my master and I was its slave. Then a gentle question appeared in my mind: Did I want to be in bondage to this master? Out loud I said "No" and this time I committed fully to break off totally the relationship-bonds, not just quit the behavior of smoking.

I was a believer in Jesus at the time and I made this choice before the Lord, and entrusted to Him the process of drug-withdrawal and learning to live without nicotine. I have been a non-smoker for the past 27 years.

I recount this story for two reasons. The first is that the Lord honored my desire to know the truth and He also revealed the character of addiction—that the inherent dynamic is one in which the addict hands his or her power to choose over to an outside power. *Addiction is actually the creation of a relationship of slave and master.* In seeing this fact and feeling how such control messed with my freedom in a very uncomfortable way, I was motivated to completely break off the relationship with smoking.

In my therapy and ministry practices, I call this "the 100% decision" and I think of it as a basic principle in dealing with addictions. I don't waste time exhorting patients to quit an addictive behavior; if they are willing, we pray to have the Holy Spirit reveal underlying beliefs by which they are attached to the power of their drug of choice. In one variation or another, the basic lie will be *I can't live without this master.* This belief needs to be uncovered, encountered, and put before the Lord, to ask for His perspective. It's not easy to give up something if, somewhere inside, you believe you can't live without it.

In our Western culture, so permeated with relativism, such a 100% decision is an unpopular and unfamiliar black-or-white choice. My experience tells me that there are important either/or choices to be made in life, and sometimes making an absolute, all-in choice makes all the difference. I first encountered such a choice when the Lord spoke to me in Michigan with the words, "I am Life" and "you must choose"— between Him and the life-supports of drugs to which I had been attached for many years. It is the choice implicit in Jesus' words: "No one can serve two masters; for either he will hate the one and serve the other, or else he will be loyal to the one and despise the other" (Matthew 6:24).

Addictions are stumbling blocks and untenable diversions in God's Kingdom because underneath the *I can't live without this master* belief is the deep hunger within the God-shaped hole in us that is satisfied by Him alone. An addiction dilutes the desire God planted in human hearts to call Him "Master" and mean it 100%: spirit, soul, and body. In biblical language, an addiction is a form of idolatry: placing anyone or anything other than God in a rulership position in a human heart.

However, often it is difficult to break off addictive relationships with behaviors, experiences, persons, or substances. And that brings up the second reason for telling my story about how I quit smoking. Severing the ties of addiction is similar to breaking off a romantic relationship: the coupling may not be working well to enhance overall health and wellbeing, but there are pleasurable aspects that are satisfying and therefore difficult to give up.

A meandering thread running throughout the narrative of my story and that of my patients and friends, is recognition of being hardwired (created) for relationship by a relationally oriented God. Love is all about relationship: giving and receiving, connecting, bonding, attaching, uniting, communing, caring. Through advances in brain science during the past 20 years, there is physical evidence of an *attachment center* in the human brain.

Patterns of attachment are established in early childhood development, with joy and pleasure linked to secure attachments to parents, and pain linked to disrupted or deficient bonding. The absence or deficiency of secure attachment creates an internal state of distress as a person grows into an adult; and then this uncomfortable state becomes a predisposition to latch onto *anything* that increases pleasure and decreases pain in the attachment center. When this latching-onto takes place (the drug of choice) it doesn't want to let go. If the drug-attachment is allowed to grow, it literally hijacks the brain and the person...and a "master" has been put on the throne. It's called addiction.

Attachment and bonding are embedded in human nature; God created us to attach to Him and to others in secure, loving, joy-filled relationships. But for many, the capacity for attachment and trust in relationships has been damaged, and the distress and anxiety of disconnection agitate for remedies wherever they can be found—looking for "love" in all the wrong places.

I told you of my early childhood isolation, in which my parents saw themselves more as my guardians until I went off to the seminary at age 14. Having a "band of brothers" in my fellow seminarians staved off the inner distress of disconnection, but when I dropped out of everything I had been part of, I was isolated and vulnerable to be "hijacked." I had almost no relationship skills or capacity, and the pain of isolation latched onto cigarettes, marijuana, alcohol, pornography, promiscuity, work-performance, and cultish communities. All of these were addictions that did not provide a healthy resolution of my attachment issues. Rather, they medicated the pain and gave some pleasure, but they did not give the joy or wellbeing that comes from authentic, growing, person-to-person relationships.

When I entered into the changing-out process of the Reconciliation, a major part of my initial healing was to break off those "relationships" and allow the Holy Spirit to replace those masters with The Master. True to His mission-statement in Luke 4:18, Jesus set my heart free from the addictive bondages that had held me captive. At first there were many lies that kept me disconnected, anxious, and feeling like an outcast; but when I finally let in the truth that my Father takes delight in me and wants me to delight in Him, healing began.

Inner Healing ministry focuses on allowing the Holy Spirit to restore a heart-to-heart connection with the God who loves us. In John 15:11 NASB, Jesus prayed "…that My joy may be in you, and that your joy may be made full." He was talking about abiding in Him as a branch in a vine…that this abiding is a path to joy. I have experienced this joy as have many of my patients and friends. In a major way, abiding and attaching to Him has begun to heal the distress of many years of detachment, and I have seen in myself and in others a growing capacity to love God and others. I am a willing "slave" of this benevolent Master, but best of all He has also called me "friend," and that brings a joy beyond words.

- **A Malevolent Myth of Masculinity**

The subject for my doctoral dissertation in clinical psychology arose from the accumulated pain of isolation that I had experienced as a man. My father had been an emotionally distant man. My dad's father had been totally absorbed in his work, and he was also emotionally distant. I am told that when my paternal grandfather retired from his railroad job he came home, climbed into bed with heavy depression, and died three months later. His work was over…his life was over. My maternal grandfather died of a brain aneurysm at age 52. I never knew my grandfathers. My "fathers" in the seminary had been taught, as were all seminarians, to avoid personal intimacy. At age 42 I was well-practiced in male relational avoidance. I had several male friends but they were not close relationships.

My dissertation was designed to shed light on why we men do not communicate at substantive levels of intimacy with one another. The sociological research showed that men relate shallowly with one another. I developed an experiential research model to demonstrate what happens in men when self-disclosing with one another.

The research instrument was a three-day workshop for men only. I co-facilitated the several sharing sessions of each workshop with a friend whom I had previously called, telling him of my shallow relationships with men. He had expressed the same problem for himself. We met for months and shared with one another events and inner feelings that we had never shared with anyone. The benefits we experienced by doing this prompted me to choose man-to-man self-disclosure as my dissertation topic.

I interviewed the men in my study, individually and in the groups of eight that comprised each of several workshops. Through interviews it became clear that *fear* was the restrictive force that limited these men from self-disclosing with one another. Some sample statements: "When I watched others opening up and being questioned, it looked like an attack. I was real afraid of that happening to me." Another man said, "At first I felt the old male comparing and competing undercurrent….I felt you all might criticize me or think I was weak or something."

However, after going through the fear-barrier and actually self-disclosing, the men had a different experience: "When my turn to share came, it was more like an embrace. It was like anything I said was being hugged. When my turn passed I realized that I hadn't been attacked." Another remarked: "Where I felt energized was in the experience of no longer being alone, and being heard and understood....It was a feeling of relief."

The walls of isolation thickly surround many men in our culture. In my practice, one of my focuses has been on men's issues, not because I am an expert—far from it. From my own life and from taking an interest in the lives of men, I know that there are myths of masculinity that strongly block and discourage us from being what we were created to be. In this section I focus on what I consider to be the most debilitating myth: *self-reliance.*

Within the concept of self-reliance are the following: independence, self-sufficiency, self-determination, individualism—basically *self-containment* on every level. In many ways men are trained up to believe that self-reliance is the hallmark of being a real man. The results of this training are individuals who are proud, arrogant, controlling, insecure, dictatorial...and they live on self-created *islands* with limited capacity to reach out relationally to others. I lived on such an island for many years.

What men are told is a merit-badge of manhood and our greatest strength (self-reliance) is actually our greatest weakness. Inside this encapsulated way of living is the pain of aloneness and insecurity that results from a lack of relational connection. Humans are relational beings; we are nourished and strengthened by giving and receiving in relationships. To have that part shut off or underdeveloped weakens us terribly.

I have had more than one man sit in my office for a first visit and tell me how wrong it felt for him to be there asking for help. Ingrained into his mind was a belief that he was supposed to deal with the problems of life on his own, by his own resources. Needing someone else to help him was perceived as a weakness to be avoided, if he wanted to retain any semblance of his manhood.

Within this belief lies the perfect atmosphere for developing addictions, *which deliver the effects of attachment and bonding, without the substance of a real relationship.* Let me demonstrate how this works.

Pornography is a drug of choice for many men to medicate the pain of their inner isolation. It is a fantasy relationship with a glossy "woman" in a magazine or video, involving an illusion of intimacy as the image "looks" into a man's eyes. He "relationally connects" by sexual stimulation and a pleasurable release of masturbation. It is a "relationship" of counterfeit attachment and counterfeit joy which pops like a bubble after the balm of excitement, pleasure, and "intimacy" momentarily soothes the painful feelings of living alone on an island. The man then feels shame, feels bad about himself, goes a little deeper into hiding, and ends up feeling more alone than before. He will then cycle back into porn to medicate the deeper loneliness. Pretty desperate stuff, but such is the vulnerability created by being-unto-oneself.

A counselor can do cognitive talk-therapy all day long and never get to the buried pain in a man. In fact, cerebral processing is the "safe" tower in which many men hide in order to avoid the emotional messiness of relational living. They live out their days within the walls of the mind. The intellect becomes a bastion of independence, opposing any move which might let down a protective guard and lead to trusting or depending on another person—including God.

Most seriously, then, the myth of self-reliance is a lie that creates a defiant opposition to acknowledge utter reliance on God. It keeps men from taking on the attitude of a dependent child that Jesus said was a condition for entering the Kingdom of Heaven (Matthew 18:3). It is a lie that Satan has been developing for a long time, and I have called it a *malevolent* myth of masculinity because of his obvious intent to use this lie to keep men from the Kingdom and weaken them for true Kingdom living. Kingdom living is *family* living, structured by the giving and receiving that is the essence of relationships.

I succumbed to the lie of self-reliance for decades. It took many blows before the walls of my false-masculine heart gave way and the Holy Spirit could come within to minister to the pain, the fear, and the uncertainty—first to my deadened spirit and then to the anxious, imprisoned captives in my soul. It has been an arduous journey to become dependent on God and able to live within the giving/receiving dynamic of human relationships. God continues to develop my capacity to relate to Him and to others.

I have included this section on men because the separation between the heads and hearts of many men is so great that many have lost connection with interior parts of themselves. They need the Holy Spirit to search their hearts, to find and rescue these abandoned parts of their souls.

Further, men have been so deceived about their identities, about what it means to be a man, that they need to make direct appeal to the Holy Spirit in the kind of personal engagement facilitated by Inner Healing ministry. One of the most powerful Inner Healings I received occurred after a long-held belief came to the surface of my mind following a time of prayer: *I didn't measure up as a man...I was deficient and lacking in manly qualities.* My facilitator asked the Lord to show me the Lord's truth. The words are still there in their gentle strength as I write about this event. "You are *My* man," came the simple yet firm reply.

During that session, something cracked open inside...perhaps a protective shell of believing I had to try harder, strive more, perform at a higher level to measure up. My heart broke open and tears of pain and relief flooded out from the memory-container. Understanding washed over me like a wave: "My manhood is in God and that I've already qualified and met the standard of measurement by being in Him." I understood in my heart that who I am is in Him, my Creator, and that He was forging my manhood now as I turned my life over to Him. And I know Jesus wants to speak this truth into the hearts of men and women alike: that our very identities are to found in Him, the perfection of human nature.

I can't speak experientially for women, but I speak as a man who has been freed from dungeon-existence on a cold, dark island. I exhort my male readers who resonate with what I have described in this section of the book: Resist the pull of the myth that tells you to keep your problems to yourselves, to work them out by yourselves, to be self-reliant. I encourage you to seek out someone who will guide you to soak in the Presence of the Lord, for only He has the power to demolish the thick walls that may be encasing your hearts. Your relationship with God depends on this healing, and there are others in your lives waiting for you to be set free to love them with your *whole hearts*: your wives, your children, your families, friends, and all whom you encounter on your journey.

In the AFTERSTORY, I suggest some resources. There is a way for men to be the men God intends us to be.

• Inner Healing for All Occasions

In this last section I want to say a few words about creating space and time in daily life for exchanges with the Master to take place. Inside the structure and steps of Inner Healing ministry is the simple relational reality of interacting with the Master. The exchanges discussed throughout this book are elements of relationship: speaking and listening, knowing and being known, receiving love and loving in return. Jesus saying "Come to Me" in Matthew 11:28 and "Abide in Me" in John 15:4 are clear invitations for intimate relationship in which burdens can be released and Life can be received. In this relationship, the mission and intention of Jesus remains the same: to destroy the works of the devil, replacing them with His character, i.e., the sheer goodness of the only sinless Man.

When I engage the Lord during a quiet time in the morning, the purpose of quieting my mind is to receive an awareness of His Presence. As I feel led, I open to a passage in the written Word and begin asking the Lord to connect me with Himself, the living Word. My desire is for Him to show me whatever He wishes me to focus on, and then to show me whatever He wants me to know about that place of focus. I seek communion with Him first, spirit to Spirit, giving permission for Him to then release His truth into my soul.

Sometimes Inner Healing moments occur during these prayer-times as the Holy Spirit reveals some part of my old, dark self that has been hanging on...not yet fully accepting that it belongs on the Cross. The release/receive dynamic takes place in these moments as I allow the Lord to make His Reconciliation-exchange in my soul. And the same exchange can and does take place in moments during the day when an ugly or afflicted part of my soul shows its face. I don't always take the time for an exchange, but when I do, relief and peace follow. And however slowly, the relationship with my Lord grows, as does His Presence within me.

I encourage you to go the Lord directly when in distress, confusion, fear, or pain—like a child running to his father and mother—seeking guidance, reassurance, and truth. All the guidelines and steps I have given can be self-administered within your relationship with your Mentor, the Holy Spirit. The questions: "Lord, what do You want to show me here?" and "Holy Spirit, I don't know what to do here, what is your guidance?" can take you through many obstacles.

If you get stuck you can have a trusted Inner Healing facilitator, minister, or friend assist you in clearing away blockages. Some lies are deeply embedded in the soul and they don't easily relinquish their hold. A trained Inner Healing facilitator would be helpful in such a case. Also, new models of Inner Healing in groups and community settings have been developed. In the AFTERSTORY I give directions to resources for individual and community-based ministries. Asking for help is sometimes the humility through which the Lord can get to the heart of the matter.

The Cross. There is a special place of meeting that I would like to share with you. In certain times in my life when I have felt ripped apart by the ravages of sin and wounds, I have met Jesus as the Crucified One. This has been the most intimate and Life-giving place of my meetings with Him. The relevant passage is from Romans 6:5, "We have been planted together in the likeness of His death." In the grafting process (such as a branch grafted into the main stem of a grapevine) the host stem is cut (wounded) in the same way as the graft. The wounded stem and the wounded graft are cut so that they fit exactly into each other, into each other's likeness, if you will. When graft and host are fit together they are then bound together with a cloth so that the inner life (sap) of the vine can flow into the grafted branch and give life to it.

Earlier in my life, whenever I heard the words of Jesus, "I am the vine, you are the branches....Abide in Me" (John 15:4,5) I pictured Jesus after the Last Supper saying those words. But I have now experienced Him sometimes as the Crucified One saying to "Abide in Me" *there, at the Cross.* "I am crucified with Christ" (Galatians 2:20).

On the Cross Jesus was wounded, and in His opened wounds a place was prepared where my wounds might be fit in and bound up in Him. In this place of meeting, of abiding, I have experienced that Jesus took on my sins and my afflictions. I can, and do, bring to Him the burden of my sins, confess them to Him, and then receive the truth that He has already taken these sins upon Himself on the Cross and disposed of them. Or I can, and do, bring the shame or pain of soul-wounds to Him and release these afflictions onto Him—knowing that there is a place in Him that is cut in exactly the shape of my wounds.

He has already specifically taken these afflictions upon Himself in the death of my old nature, which death He hosted in Himself. I let my wounds fit into Him, releasing them to Him, and then I receive His resurrected Life from Himself as the Vine.

In this releasing and receiving there has been an amazing clarification and experiential realization that Jesus' Death and Resurrection are not separate but, rather, interrelated. Further, the Crucifixion and Resurrection, which together comprise the Reconciliation, have on-going extension into the space and time of daily life in 2014...and beyond.

For me the Cross is now a *living* symbol. I encourage recipients and patients to abide in Jesus there, when the Holy Spirit opens the way to receive healing in this manner. I have also found that a Reconciliation-exchange can take place rather quickly sometimes in unstructured Inner Healing moments in daily life. For instance, a judgmental attitude towards a person may jump onto center stage in my mind in certain situations. I have felt the reality of "I have been crucified with Christ" in such a situation, and have said either to myself or aloud, "be crucified" to the attitude, and I release it. Sometimes in such a moment an image of the Cross comes to mind and, like an iron filing pulled to a magnet, the released judgmental attitude flies to the Cross, where it truly belongs.

Final Formulation

I have expended many words in writing this book, but there is simplicity to the Inner Healing experience. Jesus' heart is full of healing compassion for us all the time. Whoever opens up to Him in faith is drawn into His healing Presence in which broken hearts are made whole and the pain of aloneness is vanquished. And this is true for one's past, present, and future experiences.

Inner Healing ministry mostly focuses on His Presence in the *past* experiences of our lives. But Inner Healing, as a continuing *present* action of the Reconciliation, can occur in a morning meditation in which one becomes aware of an ungodly belief and surrenders it to God. Inner Healing can take place in any moment in daily living when a person prays for the Holy Spirit to reveal thoughts that are out of alignment with His will—then releases what is revealed and receives the Holy Spirit's replacement into that vacated place in the heart.

Also, I have experienced peace in myself and in patients through asking the Lord to help perceive His Presence in *future* situations. One of my patients had a phobia of public speaking. He focused on the Lord's Presence with him while imagining himself training a large group of employees in an upcoming presentation. His sense of God's Presence stayed with him during the actual presentation and he had no fear. He was amazed and encouraged.

In summary, perhaps a succinct way to express Inner Healing is to say that it is the practice of walking in the Presence of the Holy Spirit at all times.

Finally, I invite you all to take encouragement and hope from these words:

And I am convinced and sure of this very thing, that He who began a good work in you will continue until the day of Jesus Christ, right up to the time of His return, developing that good work, and perfecting and bringing it to full completion in you.

(Philippians 1:6 Amplified Bible)

Afterword: A New Horizon

Throughout this book, I have asserted that humans are created as relational beings, primarily to be in a Life-relationship with God, and secondarily, yet significantly, to be in loving relationships with one another. A further assertion is that the breach in our relationship with God has been a collective trauma for the entire human race. This trauma has cut us off from Life and has plunged us into all the separation anxiety, ultra self-absorption, and disintegration this world has known. Healing is making-whole, and wholeness begins with re-attachment to God.

While finishing up my book, I read Curt Thompson's *Anatomy of the Soul*. As a neuroscientist and psychiatrist, he sees the relational nature of the human brain reflecting the relational nature of humankind. He presents the ever-growing evidence that all parts of the brain seek to work together in harmonious, integrated ways...*and* brains seek to interact with *other* brains. Dr. Thompson bluntly declares that neurons don't exist in isolated states; by nature they are interactive.

He goes on to say that gathering information is an important function in life, and the left hemisphere of the brain is adept at developing storehouses that provide the structures of logic and sound reason for daily living. But we also need the sensory, non-verbal, emotional processing of our brain's right hemisphere to anchor us in fully experiencing reality. When functioning together, left and right lobes in harmony, a more accurate perception of reality occurs. Dr. Thompson gives the image of needing the rudder of a left brain...but without the flowing, experiential current of the right brain, our boats aren't going anywhere.

This evidence from neuroscience confirms the integrative approach of Inner Healing ministry and therapy. When there is access to right-brain experiential knowing, and this mode blends with the left-brain mode, deeper healing takes place.

However, the restoration realized through Inner Healing exchanges may need assistance in repairing damage and filling in deficits from having spent many years in patterned relational detachment. Looking at the stages of human development (infant, child, adolescent, adult, elder) I can see several areas in my own development in which growth towards maturity was sadly lacking. In addition to Inner Healing, I need relational maturity skills to fill in some big gaps. I have been seeking help from colleagues who are equipped for this mentoring.

My story is one of having multiple insecure attachments. The breakthrough-connections that happened in my Inner Healing created a secure attachment at the deepest level—with God, and I nourish this attachment daily by engaging with God. But I, like many others, need coaching and training for how to attach to others in healthy ways. Learning to live in community is difficult enough these days as daily we are being trained to interact with technology instead of with people. Increasingly, it takes intentional actions to cultivate wholesome community.

I become more *spiritually mature* as I grow closer to God and develop His character within me; I grow in *human maturity* as I learn to relate to others with competence. On yet another level of synchronization, these aspects of maturity can work together in an integrated way on the journey to wholeness. And by developing both forms of maturity, we shape both facets of our deeply-embedded human character: to be dependent on God and interdependent with one another.

After finishing *Healing Troubled Hearts*, I learned of a ministry, Healing Center International, whose vision is to draw together models of individual Inner Healing with the more group-based models of healing and relational maturity. The website is GodHealsToday.org. I plan on exploring this ministry soon to discover how a variety of models can synchronize with one another to facilitate full healing.

As I continue to grow into the person God intends me to be, I become more mindful of how life-sustaining is the interactive time I spend with God and with others. More and more I feel *loving interaction* as intrinsic to the very nature of God and man. The inter-changeability of *Life* and *Love* comes into sharper focus, experientially, while the false identity of solo-Bill continues to fade, like mist dispersing in the morning sun.

Please feel free to write to me at <u>billday@healingtroubledhearts.com</u>, or visit me on my website: <u>healingtroubledhearts.com</u>. Thank you for spending your valuable time reading this book.

Bill Day

AFTERSTORY

The Shaping of *Healing Troubled Hearts*

Introduction

In this final section I tell the story of the people, the events, and the resources which have been influential and formative in my life. The book has flowed out of my life experiences...as such, the shape of my book is congruent with the shape of my life. I have chosen the format of a storyline as the way of presenting what might otherwise be called *references, acknowledgments*, and *bibliography*. I hope that a narrative description will be not only more lively but also more accurate.

Chapter 1. When I was in my thirties, bumbling through life with emotional pain poking me all over, I blamed my sorry state on a cruel, uncaring God. I believed that He had set me up in life with weird, super-devout Irish Catholic parents who had hijacked me from the very start of my life and had brainwashed me into believing that my destiny in life was to be a Roman Catholic priest. Decades later, after I placed my life in God's hands, affirming that He has always had a good and wise plan for me, I was able to receive the blessings that have come from my family of origin.

My father was an intelligent man who loved my mother dearly and provided a secure home for his family by his work and his character. He had a reputation in our town for being a man of his word. At one time I critically dismissed my father as simplistic and naïve; now I hope that every smidgen of his humility passed on to me, father to son, and that it will flow generously into the inner layers of my soul.

My mother was a teacher and a gifted musician, but she was first of all a dedicated Christian and a homemaker. I can still hear her Irish laughter ringing out in our home. I visited her on a regular basis in her later years and we formed a relationship in which I experienced her love as mother to son, instead of guardian to a priest-to-be.

My older brother Tom died three years ago. He had been a quadriplegic for 33 years after a car accident. I didn't know him in my early years but developed a close friendship with him in the decade before his death. His is a story of amazing perseverance and I learned many life-lessons from him. His autobiography, *Hidden Handicaps*, documents his incredible adventure.

My older sister Kay and my younger brother Pat are now good friends of mine. My sister's love has been a reassuring thread of connection throughout my life. She held onto loving me and being there for me during times when I was anything but loveable.

Pat is writing his third book and is giving me valuable assistance as I write my first. My close friendship with him has been a key factor in making it through some crushingly low points in my life. I grow closer to my sister and brother as the years go by.

Looking at the whole panorama of my life and how it has unfolded, I have only gratitude for each one in my family of origin. I now believe that God, as Lovingkindness, wisely knew what He was doing from the start.

The analogy of the arrows in this chapter is from *The Sacred Romance*, by Brent Curtis and John Eldredge, p. 19. This is one my favorite books about God's multifaceted character in the dynamic of wounding and healing. John is adept at tuning into the hearts of men in our culture, pointing out the importance of men relating more significantly with God and with one another. His website is: ransomedheart.com.

Chapter 2. Desperation, pain, and chronic anxiety are not usually thought of as sought-after shaping forces, but they have a mission. All of them drove me to move beyond my status quo. From age 21-42, I ran from one desperate state to another, moved along by continual emotional pain and an undercurrent of anxiety.

Liberal Catholic theology, humanistic psychology, drugs, and New Age spirituality were formative forces, but none of them resolved the turmoil in my soul. Each phase became a "not this" and I moved on, driven by the desperation of being totally lost.

Chapter 3. Beginning in this chapter and sprinkled throughout the book are quotes from and references to the Bible. I grew up in a Roman Catholic culture, and one of the doctrines poured into my head was that the Bible was God's Word, end of story. Later, as a liberal theologian, I examined the historical details of much of the Bible and decided it was a mixture of human and divine authorship, allowing for more subjective interpretation; I made it say whatever I wanted it to say. Later still, as a humanistic psychologist, I considered the Bible to be just one of many classics of human literature.

Fast-forwarding to my post-conversion years, I have a memory of myself, sitting at a kitchen table with an opened Bible in front of me. I was confused and conflicted but I wanted to know the truth: Was this book in front of me God's Word? Did He speak through it? Three years previously, I had an encounter with God and knew He was real. So there at the kitchen table I poured out my heart to Him, asking Him to show me the truth as to whether or not the Bible was really inspired by Him.

What happened next is difficult to explain. I felt an inward nudge to begin reading the Scripture in front of me—the Book of Isaiah in the Old Testament. I began reading one of the verses and immediately was in a new, never-experienced-before dimension of interacting with a book. I had a clear sense of a personal presence speaking the words to me, much as if a person were sitting there talking to me. As I was reading, the words came alive. Someone alive was speaking the verses to me.

My confusion began to lift. My question was being answered. In full-hearted prayer, there at the kitchen table, I had been talking to God, asking Him for a response. I sensed that He was speaking the words in Isaiah as a response to my questions. I asked and had received. Peace began to replace my anguish, and from that day until today I have believed that the Bible is God's inspired Word. I drink of it daily and experience its refreshing truths.

Since that day I have tested the contents of the Bible many times by accepting what it says and then acting on it. Now I *know* it as the Word of God because of the depth of truth I have experienced and tested. Also, on several occasions while meditating on the Word, I have had that same kitchen-table experience of the words coming alive, speaking from that same mysterious, personal Presence.

Chapter 5. A significant bottoming out occurred in the last three years of the century. The Fellowship of Christ was a spiritual hospital for me during this time. I thank God for many in the church who gave unstintingly of their time, their prayer, and their care. The compassion I experienced from them and several close friends had a shaping effect upon me. Because of their care I know more convincingly in my heart that love heals, restores, and brings hope. Thanks to all of you: the "doctors," "nurses," "surgical assistants," and compassionate care-givers. I would have wasted away without you.

Isaiah 61 Ministry is an Inner Healing ministry within the Fellowship of Christ. Anyone can sign up for healing prayer sessions. They are a fully equipped team who also offer training for Inner Healing. This ministry can be found at <u>fellowshipofchrist.org</u>. They facilitate Inner Healing in ways that most closely resemble the approach I have outlined in this book. This is my close-knit band of brothers and sisters, and I thank God for them. They inspire me to listen closely to the Holy Spirit.

Chapter 6. In the early years after 2000, I learned some basic principles of Inner Healing ministry through the work of Dr. Ed Smith and Theophostic Prayer Ministry. He was my first mentor and remains to this day a foundational source for understanding the dynamics of lie-based thinking. His *Basic Training Seminar* and his training DVDs are part of the core curriculum for our Isaiah 61 Ministry at Fellowship of Christ. His guidelines for facilitators are the most comprehensive I have seen. This ministry can be found at: <u>theophostic.com</u>. On this site you will be able to locate certified prayer ministers worldwide, as well as many training resources.

During these years, our ministry team also delved into learning how to hear God's voice and commune with Him through the writings of Mark Virkler. He continues to deepen the understanding and practice of healing prayer. His training and teaching can be found at:

cwgministries.org. This is an excellent resource for anyone who has difficulty hearing from God in the interactive dialogue of prayer.

Chapter 7. My second major mentor is Father Andrew Miller, an Episcopal priest and a licensed clinical social worker. I have done Fr. Andrew's training and received healing through him. His methods are a mainstay in my therapy practice and in Isaiah 61 Ministry as well.

Fr. Andrew has a gifted capacity to come alongside patients with compassion and understanding. He has taught me much about listening with the heart and mind of Jesus. Also, through him I discovered the advances in neuroscience that help in understanding how humans process emotional trauma. Training seminars and information on his ministry can be found on his website: heartsyncministries.org.

My third major mentor for Inner Healing ministry and therapy is Dr. Karl Lehman, a Christian psychiatrist. The Immanuel approach of Dr. Lehman has effective principles that I have blended into my own therapeutic approach. He offers training and has a referral directory of facilitators on his website: immanuelapproach.com. I recommend that you check out his resources and read some of the many articles he has written.

Dr. Lehman is also involved in joint projects with Dr. James Wilder, Ed Khouri, and others who have developed a model of healing that combines biblical wisdom with brain science. Their work offers understanding of, and steps towards, relational and spiritual maturity—especially in groups and community settings. Contact info: lifemodelworks.org; thrivetoday.org.

Chapter 8. The reference for SOZO Ministry is: bethelsozo.com. I have not trained in this ministry but the Inner Healing session administered to me was very effective and I plan to visit the Bethel community in California next year. Healing and training are offered through this ministry.

Chapter 9. The quote from Billy Graham comes from Lee Strobel as a crusade attendee. He gives his account in his book, *The Case for Faith*,

p. 7. I enjoy the investigative nature of Lee's books, and especially appreciate *The Case for Christ* and the *Case for the Real Jesus*.

Chapter 10. DeVern Fromke, *Ultimate Intention*, has plumbed significant scriptural depths regarding the heart of God for His creation. Fromke has been a vital resource for understanding the relational nature of God.

The article on "reconciliation" in the *International Standard Bible Encyclopedia* illumined my understanding of the scriptural kinship between exchange and reconciliation. This excellent article was written by Geoffrey W. Bromiley, one of the editors of the four-volume Encyclopedia. Additionally, Bromiley's entry on "psychology" was an eye-opening examination of the difference between theological and scientific psychology. I have a greater understanding of my calling in life by reading his article.

Chapter 11. Eastern mysticism is a main component of New Age teaching. In several books and DVDs, John Ankerberg has expressed succinct but clear differences between Christianity and the Eastern worldview. His analyses confirm what I learned and practiced during my 15 years living in the occult realm. His website is: johnankerberg.org. Also helpful in understanding New Age spiritualities are the writings of Peter Jones. His website: truthxchange.com.

The footnote reference is to Oswald Chambers, *My Utmost for His Highest*, July 12. Oswald Chambers' meditations speak to the process of spiritual maturation. I read him daily.

Chapter 12. I quote Watchman Nee in Volume One of his three-volume work, *The Spiritual Man.* Watchman Nee has been one of my spiritual mentors because he writes so personally and thoroughly about what it means to live a full life in Christ. He is a man of the spirit in a way that encompasses the soul and body as well. He is full of passion and heart, and has carefully stayed true to the Spirit of the Word. Nee's intent is always to reveal more of his Master, the Lord Jesus. I consider *The Spiritual Man* a masterpiece.

I also reference Chester and Betsy Kylstra, husband-wife pioneers in the ministry of Inner Healing. I especially benefitted from their understanding of generational transmission of tendencies towards iniquity, and I know individuals who have received healing in their residential ministry near the mountains of North Carolina. The word-study referenced is in their book, *Restoring the Foundations*, pp. 407-413. Their website is: rtfi.org.

Chapter 13. Dallas Willard wrote *Hearing God* to biblically anchor his wife's Inner Healing ministry. In this book he handles the complex issues involved in conversational prayer with God. Dr. Willard's grasp of the nature of the living Word has given voice to what I believe and have wanted to express in my book. A prolific writer and speaker, Dallas Willard died in 2013. He will be missed by many.

Chapter 14. The quotes from A.W. Tozer are from his book, *Born After Midnight*, as excerpted by Warren Wiersbe in *The Best of A.W. Tozer*. His thoughts on a sanctified imagination are Tozer's usual laser beams cutting to the core of an issue. His books and sermons are always well worth the read.

Leanne Payne, *Restoring the Christian Soul*, is another pioneer in the development of Inner Healing ministry. I spent a week with her in one of her healing prayer retreats and came away with personal healing plus training applicable to my ministry and therapy practice. She and her Pastoral Care Ministries can be found at: leannepayne.org.

Chapter 15 and Chapter 16. Recently I have been introduced to the work of David Takle by reading his book, *The Truth About Lies and Lies About Truth*. His approach is similar to mine in understanding what works and what doesn't work in spiritual formation. Our church home-group is currently studying his video course, *Forming*—an excellent resource for learning how to engage with God individually and in a group setting. This course is part of *Thriving: Recover your Life* series from thrivetoday.org. David can be found at: kingdomformation.org.

Chapter 18. My discussion of inner child is based on the biblical exegesis of David Seamands, in *Healing of Memories*. Dr. Seamands has written extensively about Inner Healing, especially focusing on how our emotions are damaged by lies and trauma. His writings have many case-studies that illustrate his approach.

An earlier work, *Healing for Damaged Emotions*, received judgment from online vigilante groups who scan writings for "psychoheresy." Basically I have found his material to be therapeutically and biblically sound. I recommend that you read him and decide for yourselves.

Many authors already named have come under fire from critics. My adaptation of methods and principles of inner healing from various sources is not necessarily an endorsement of the whole body of work of any particular author. I ask you to read what I have written and to evaluate it on its own merits, rather than as representative of any specific stream or method.

Chapter 19. These are verbatim stories from persons who have received one or more Inner Healing sessions during the past 15 years. I am grateful to my patients for all you have taught me: by the authentic ways you have wrestled with issues and by sharing with me your intimate dialogues with the Lord. Thank you for trusting me to walk with you into some scary, vulnerable places. You are daily inspirations to me. I am a better man for having known you.

Chapter 22. Some of my approach to dealing with the demonic comes from the afore-mentioned teaching of Ed Smith. Also helpful has been *Deep Wounds, Deep Healing*, by Charles H. Kraft.

For the section on addiction, I refer you to a resource already listed: thrivetoday.org. The brain-science folks understand what is going on with addiction, especially in the context of what an addict is missing in human and spiritual development.

Regarding the section on masculinity, my dissertation published in 1987 was titled: *Man to Man: A Phenomenological Investigation of the Experience of Self-Disclosure among Men*. Although I have grown out of and beyond much of the worldview I had then, the intense project with those men definitely had a shaping influence on my life. Closer to my current view of masculinity is *Wild at Heart*, by John Eldredge, and *Healing the Masculine Soul*, by Gordon Dalbey.

A reference for the final section of this chapter is Andrew Murray, one of my all-time favorite authors. Much of what I express throughout the book about Jesus' image of vine and branches (John 15) comes from soaking in the devotional writing of Andrew Murray. He spent several seasons working in a vineyard in order to become familiar with all the particulars of grapevine farming: planting, pruning, grafting, harvesting. Then he wrote two books—*The True Vine* and *Abide in Christ*—that are simple yet profound explications of Jesus' words in John 15. Andrew Murray is a spiritual giant, yet an extraordinarily humble man. He is one of my heroes.

One of my heroines is the author of historical fiction, BJ Hoff. She plumbs amazing spiritual depths through her stories and characters, and is the finest wordsmith in her genre of literature I have encountered. Towards the end of her novella, *The Penny Whistle*, there is a beautiful, God-orchestrated Inner Healing session with the main character, Jonathan Stewart. I heartily recommend this novella and all the writings of BJ Hoff, at bjhoff.com.

Final Acknowledgments

I am a blessed man because I have a Circle of Friends: 25 colleagues and friends who have been reading drafts of this book and have been encouraging me with their prayers and critiques. I thank you for your time and for the loan of your minds and hearts. I couldn't have done this without you.

I am a blessed man because I belong to a group of healing prayer ministers at Fellowship of Christ. God continues my healing through the sense of belonging I have with all of you, as well as the sense of belonging I have with our whole church family.

I am a blessed man because I have three remarkable sons, Adam, Adrian, and John, all of whom are coming into the fullness of their manhood. Guys, I hope to stay vigorous in the years to come so I can stand shoulder to shoulder with you as you make your way through life. Thank you for your love and your forgiveness—both are precious to me. And I am also blessed because, added to the mix are Laurie and Matt, who came aboard alongside my wife ten years ago. I am truly enjoying getting to know you as we share family times together; thanks for accepting me so warmly. I hope to see the five of you more in upcoming years...and our grandchildren (we now have three beautiful girls).

I am a blessed man because God has given me a precious wife who is so much to me...yet she is first of all a woman who has found her identity in the Lord. Her first desire is to please her Father in all that she is and does, and then her heart is for her husband, our children, our grandchildren, and all others. She is known in our Fellowship as a generous and joyful person. I am a blessed man to have you, SusieQ. You are the best answer to prayer I could have received. Thanks for your love and patience (not to mention your exquisite editing skills) during these past two years.

Final Prayer

Thank you, Holy Spirit, for Your constant companionship during the months of completing this project. You have been a faithful Friend in guiding and sustaining me. You have steadied my hand and put boldness into my heart. I hope that I have been a useful instrument in Your Hands. May your mighty Wind blow through all I have written, separating the wheat from the chaff. May the chaff drift away and may the seeds of Your Truth fall into readied hearts, that Your intentions and purposes may be realized in all ages to come.

Bibliography: Select Resources from Whom I Have Drawn Wisdom

Anderson, Neil T. *Victory over the Darkness.* Ventura, CA: Regal Books, 1990.

Bromiley, G.W. (ed.) *The International Standard Bible Encyclopedia.* Grand Rapids, MI: Wm. B. Eerdmans Publishing, 1979.

Chambers, Oswald. *My Utmost for His Highest.* Grand Rapids, MI: Discovery House, 1992.

Cowman, L.B. *Streams in the Desert*. Grand Rapids: Zondervan, 1996.

Dalbey, Gordon. *Healing the Masculine Soul*. Dallas: Word Publishing, 1988.

Day, Thomas. *Hidden Handicaps: Redemption and Triumph*. Amazon.com, 2009.

Eldredge, John, and Brent Curtis. *The Sacred Romance*. Nashville, TN: Thomas Nelson, 1997.

Fromke, DeVern. *Ultimate Intention*. Indianapolis, IN: Sure Foundation, 1963.

Guyon, Jeanne. *Experiencing the Depths of Jesus Christ*. Sargent, Georgia: Christian Books Publishing House, 1975.

Hoff, BJ. *The Penny Whistle*. Minneapolis, MN: Bethany House, 1996.

Jones, Peter. *One or Two: Seeing a World of Difference*. Escondido, CA: Main Entry Editions, 2010.

Keller, Timothy. *King's Cross*. New York: Penguin Group, 2011.

Kraft, Charles H. *Deep Wounds, Deep Healing*. Ventura, CA: Regal Books, 1993.

Kylstra, Chester and Betsy. *Restoring the Foundations*. Santa Rosa Beach, FL: Proclaiming His Word, 2001.

Lehman, Karl. *Outsmarting Yourself*. Libertyville, IL: This Joy! Books, 2011.

Lewis, C.S. *Mere Christianity*. Riverside, NJ: Macmillan Publishing, 1952.

McGrath, Johanna and Alister. *Self-Esteem: the Cross and Christian Confidence*. Wheaton, IL: Crossway Books, 2002.

Murray, Andrew. *Abide in Christ*. New Kensington, PA: Whitaker House, 1979.

Murray, Andrew. *The True Vine*. Chicago: Moody Publishers, 2007.

Murray, John. *Redemption Accomplished and Applied*. Grand Rapids: Eerdmans Publishing, 1955.

Nee, Watchman. *The Normal Christian Life*. Fort Washington, PA: Christian Literature Crusade, 1957.

Nee, Watchman. *The Spiritual Man*. New York: Christian Fellowship publishers, 1977.

Omartian, Stormie. *Lead Me, Holy Spirit*. Eugene, OR: Harvest House, 2012.

Payne, Leanne. *Restoring the Christian Soul.* Grand Rapids: Baker Books, 1991.

Sandford, John and Paula. *The Transformation of the Inner Man.* Tulsa, OK: Victory House, 1982.

Seamands, David A. *Healing Your Heart of Painful Emotions.* New York: Inspirational Press, 1993.

Smith, Edward M. *Theophostic Basic Training Seminar Manual.* Campbellsville, KY: New Creation, 2007.

Smith, Warren. *The Light that Was Dark.* Magalia, CA: Mountain Stream Press, 2005.

Stanley, Charles. *Emotions.* New York: Howard Books, 2013.

Strobel, *The Case for Faith.* Grand Rapids: Zondervan, 2000.

Takle, David. *The Truth About Lies and Lies About Truth.* Pasadena: Shepherd's House, 2008.

Tapscott, Betty. *Inner Healing Through Healing of Memories.* Kingwood, TX: Hunter Publishing, 1975.

Thompson, Curt. *Anatomy of the Soul.* Carol Stream, IL: Tyndale House, 2010.

Wiersbe, Warren (ed.). *The Best of A.W. Tozer.* Grand Rapids: Baker Books, 1978.

Wilder, E. James, Edward M. Khouri, et al. *Joy Starts Here.* East Peoria, IL: Shepherd's House, 2013.

Willard, Dallas. *Hearing God.* Downers Grove, IL: Intervarsity Press, 1999.

Creative Arts and Healing
[Comments about the cover]

The cover of this book is a painting by Kathy Ammon titled *Healing Heart*. The painting was commissioned by Bill Day and depicts an actual moment of receiving Inner Healing from the Lord Jesus. First came several discussions about Inner Healing. Then brushstrokes were prayerfully created by Kathy to capture the releasing and receiving dynamic that takes place in an exchange with the Master.

Healing Heart is a visual reminder of the healing embrace of Jesus: wrapping us in His love...removing darkness and restoring us in His light...transforming us into fullness of life in Him. The hand reaching upward is significant: we must be willing to open our hearts and receive the peace He so freely gives to those who ask.

The visual art of the cover and the written text of the book join together in tangibly expressing the ministry of Inner Healing. Such collaboration is an example of the mission of Threshold Arts Gathering, a ministry founded by Kathy Ammon. The ministry's vision is to cultivate a collaborative arts community which glorifies God, deepens faith, and provides healing transformation—bringing the love and light of Christ into full expression through the arts. For more information go to thresholdartsgathering.com.

Kathy Ammon is an accomplished artist whose life and art were transformed by a profound renewal of faith she experienced in the year 2000. She carries strong vision for revealing the sacred in human relationships through themes of love, faith and community. Her studio is located in Apex, NC. Paintings and prints are available at: kathyammon.com. Her email is kathy@kathyammon.com.

Special thanks to Anthony Holder, good friend and connoisseur of the arts, who made possible the commissioning of this painting.

Are you weary of going from one self-help book to another, looking for solutions to your emotional struggles?

Have you given up hope that your heart can be healed?

In *Healing Troubled Hearts* you may find direction and resources that will restore hope for real healing. Here is a reader who found this to be true:

I've read many books throughout my academic and consulting careers and rank Dr. Bill Day's *Healing Troubled Hearts through Exchanges with the Master* among the very best! Not only is it well written and thought-provoking; it literally has the power to change lives. The entire topic of inner healing is thoughtfully and logically explained—with a solid connection to Biblical Scripture as its foundation. Bill clearly and authoritatively describes what inner healing is and what it is not—and by interweaving his personal experiences in a humble and unpretentious way, the reader palpably knows this is a message of truth. In my opinion, it is not an overstatement to claim that this work is divinely inspired. Anyone who carries with them even a minor emotional scar from the past will be blessed by this book's contents!

Jeffrey D. E. Jeffries, Ph.D., PE, president, Paradigm Consulting Services, Inc.

CPSIA information can be obtained at www.ICGtesting.com
Printed in the USA
BVOW02s1750120514

352916BV00003B/10/P